IT TAKES A LAMB!

IT TAKES A LAMB!

An Assessment of the Profoundness of the Lord's Supper
andthe Anguish of Calvary

By Randall J. Marshall DA. DMn. ThD.

XULON ELITE

Xulon Press Elite
2301 Lucien Way #415
Maitland, FL 32751
407.339.4217
www.xulonpress.com

Unless otherwise indicated, Scripture quotations taken from the King James Version (KJV) – public domain

Printed in the United States of America.

ISBN-13: 9781545622711

Preface

Our Lord gave two ordinances to the New Testament church to observe. They are the Baptism and the Lord's Supper. We have complied with the ordinance of Baptism considerably well. There is however a transcendent failure to understand the full significance of commemorating the Lord's Supper these days. The failure to comprehend the fascinating details of the Lord's Supper is to not understand the gospel clearly. There are profound aspects that once acquired in our mind, will generate exaltation in our souls! It is my endeavor to give a closer, more profuse observation to this glorious ordinance, and obtain the depth and fullness of its blessing!

It is relevant to make you aware that this book actually began as a series of sermons, or teachings on the subject of the passion and death of Christ. Each chapter was an individual sermon that would stand on its own. As an introduction to each sermon (or chapter) I did give brief references to the aforementioned discourse. My prayer and hope is that the information you receive in these pages will overflow in your heart. The result will be to proclaim glory in the cross and the finished work of redemption!

> "But God forbid that I should glory, save in the cross of our Lord Jesus Christ, by whom the world is crucified unto me, and I unto the world." Galatians 6:14

Dedication

I respectfully dedicate this book to the memory of my father and hero, Evangelist Doctor Bob Marshall. He instilled in me the necessity to "study to show thyself approved . . ." He taught me that there are two things that are essential to acquire a good delivery.

1. Study – "Know your subject, son. Have something worth saying."
2. Be filled with the Holy Ghost! Procure excitement about what you're preaching. "If you're not excited about it son, your congregation won't be."

Apportion is also given to the memory of my grandfather, Roy Marshall. He taught me that "a good name is rather to be chosen than great riches." He also taught me that character defines the man. Grandpa had no education, but he had good, solid country values. He could neither read nor write, but he esteemed knowledge and instruction. When I was about to leave home and go to Bible college, grandpa's last instruction to me continues to ring in my ears. He said, "Son, don't let that education you're going for ruin your preaching. The next time I hear you I want you to be preaching like the building's on fire and hell is at the back door!" Grandpa went on to Heaven, but every once in a while, I look up and say, "Grandpa, I'm still preaching like you told me to!"

Special Annotation

I wish to express my deepest love and gratitude to my beloved wife Margie. Thank you Sweetheart, for all your encouragement, your patience, and your listening ear. We've weathered storms and climbed the rocky hills together. We've walked this journey hand-in-hand, never giving up or looking back. Thank you for your love, your support and your adulation for the Lord . . . and thank you for just being there. My "heart doth safely trust in you, and I value you far above rubies!" (Proverbs 31:10-31)

Acknowledgement

I aspire to propose sincere gratitude to my close friend Robert Justice, whose time, fortitude, and assistance are so greatly appreciated. My you be explicitly blessed for your aid in getting this book to publication.

The entirety of this attestation is founded on a diligent and intense study of the passover, from the Old Testament story of the deliverance by the blood of a slain lamb, to the New Testament command of our Lord to the church purchased with His own blood to "keep the feast . . . forever . . . till He come."

Exodus 12:1-14

1 And the Lord spake unto Moses and Aaron in the land of Egypt saying,

2 This month shall be unto you the beginning of months: it shall be the first month of the year to you.

3 Speak ye unto all the congregation of Israel, saying, In the tenth day of this month they shall take to them every man a lamb, according to the house of their fathers, a lamb for an house:

4 And if the household be too little for the lamb, let him and his neighbour next unto his house take it according to the number of the souls; every man according to his eating shall make your count for the lamb.

5 Your lamb shall be without blemish, a male of the first year: ye shall take it out from the sheep, or from the goats:

6 And ye shall keep it up until the fourteenth day of the same month: and the whole assembly of the congregation of Israel shall kill it in the evening.

7 And they shall take of the blood, and strike it on the two side posts and on the upper door post of the houses, wherein they shall eat it.

8 And they shall eat the flesh in that night, roast with fire, and unleavened bread; and with bitter herbs they shall eat it.

9 Eat not of it raw, nor sodden at all with water, but roast with fire; his head with his legs, and with the purtenance thereof.

10 And ye shall let nothing of it remain until the morning; and that which remaineth of it until the morning ye shall burn with fire.

11 And thus shall ye eat it; with your loins girded, your shoes on your feet, and your staff in your hand; and ye shall eat it in haste: it is the Lord's passover.

12 For I will pass through the land of Egypt this night, and will smite all the firstborn in the land of Egypt, both man and beast; and against all the gods of Egypt I will execute judgment: I am the Lord.

13 And the blood shall be to you for a token upon the houses where ye are: and when I see the blood, I will pass over you, and the plague shall not be upon you to destroy you, when I smite the land of Egypt.

14 And this day shall be unto you for a memorial; and ye shall keep it a feast to the Lord throughout your generations; ye shall keep it a feast by an ordinance for ever.

Exodus 12:24-27

24 And ye shall observe this thing for an ordinance to thee and to thy sons for ever.

25 And it shall come to pass, when ye be come to the land which the Lord will give you, according as he hath promised, that ye shall keep this service.

26 And it shall come to pass, when your children shall say unto you, What mean ye by this service?

27 That ye shall say, It is the sacrifice of the Lord's passover, who passed over the houses of the children of Israel in Egypt, when he smote the Egyptians, and delivered our houses. And the people bowed the head and worshipped.

1 Corinthians 11:17-30

17 Now in this that I declare unto you I praise you not, that ye come together not for the better, but for the worse.

18 For first of all, when ye come together in the church, I hear that there be divisions among you; and I partly believe it.

19 For there must be also heresies among you, that they which are approved may be made manifest among you.

20 When ye come together therefore into one place, this is not to eat the Lord's supper.

21 For in eating every one taketh before other his own supper: and one is hungry, and another is drunken.

22 What? have ye not houses to eat and to drink in? or despise ye the church of God, and shame them that have not? what shall I say to you? shall I praise you in this? I praise you not.

23 For I have received of the Lord that which also I delivered unto you, that the Lord Jesus the same night in which he was betrayed took bread:

24 And when he had given thanks, he brake it, and said, Take, eat: this is my body, which is broken for you: this do in remembrance of me.

25 After the same manner also he took the cup, when he had supped, saying, this cup is the new testament in my blood: this do ye, as oft as ye drink it, in remembrance of me.

26 For as often as ye eat this bread, and drink this cup, ye do shew the Lord's death till he come.

27 Wherefore whosoever shall eat this bread, and drink this cup of the Lord, unworthily, shall be guilty of the body and blood of the Lord.

28 But let a man examine himself, and so let him eat of that bread, and drink of that cup.

29 For he that eateth and drinketh unworthily, eateth and drinketh damnation to himself, not discerning the Lord's body.

30 For this cause many are weak and sickly among you, and many sleep.

Forward

"Forward," that's a good word to describe this book. We need more forward thinking, and Dr. Randall Marshall has been a student of the Bible for many years and has written this fine book as a forward thinker. He has chosen to write this book to help you and me move forward in what we know. In the world in which we live there are many conceptions and misconceptions regarding the Lord's Supper; how and when to take it properly. Dr. Marshall has some God given insight for you and me in this area. Aren't you a little curious as to how we're instructed to take Communion and to take it Scripturally? I know, I was! The best part of this book is that it is Scripturally based! It isn't supposition and tales around the pews, it's backed by Scripture after Scripture, "precept upon precept, precept upon precept, line upon line, line upon line." (Isaiah 28:10)

My prayer is that God open your mind and attune your heart to His leading as you read the book you now have in your hands! As I mentioned before, reading this book will lead you forward. Thus, forward you must go and find out more about the Lord's Supper! You'll learn something new, I guarantee it! So what are you waiting for? Go forward!

Robert H. Justice
BA. Foreign Language Ed.

Table of Contents

Chapter 1

The Observance of the Lord's Supper

1 Corinthians 11:17–30
1 Corinthians 5:6-8
Matthew 26:18-29
Exodus 12:1–14, 21-27

We are about to enter into one of the most serious, and hallowed studies that we have ever, or ever will study, in the Bible. I want to encourage each of you to pay close and strict attention during these times of study together, for we will be, by the grace of God, discussing some things which perhaps most of you have never observed in the Scripture concerning the Lord's Supper! The Lord's Supper is one of the most misunderstood ordinances in the Church today!

The thing that has bothered me for years is the seeming haphazard way in which our churches observe the Lord's Supper! How many times have you heard someone say, "Oh, all they're having is the Lord's Supper. Let's go hear the singing group instead." Or "We've been promising Uncle John and Aunt Sue we'd come and visit with them. Let's just go there instead!" The Lord's Supper has lost the greatness of its importance, because of the way our post reformation churches have handled it. Much of this can be attributed to the Paganistic holidays of the Catholics which have not only affected, but crept into our modern worship. Our Modern Holidays for the most part have a Paganistic background, that was adapted to "Christianity" by the Catholic Church!

Now I will present some things during this study, that may be new to you, but I plead with you, accept the truth, for the truth shall set you free! Do you want to learn? Do you want to grow in the knowledge of truth? Are you interested in what God's Word has to say? Even if it challenges your traditions?

I say again, one of the most misunderstood ordinances of the church is the Lord's Supper! And to misunderstand the Lord's Supper is to not understand the gospel clearly!

Paul told the Corinthians that in their coming together for the Lord's Supper, they were not coming together for the better, but for the worse! And I believe it's so in our churches today! Paul went on to say, the Lord had revealed some things to Him concerning the Lord's Supper. It was to be observed in proper order, and not to be entered into unworthily! I do feel we could use the same instruction today!

As we introduce this study, there are three words, or phrases, I want us to get a proper understanding of. The definition of these words is very important as we journey through this study of the Lord's Supper.

1. "In Remembrance of Me" means a memorial, or 'as a memorial.'
2. "Unworthily" means "haphazardly," and is speaking of the manner in which it (the Service – the Memorial) is entered into.

3. "Feast" doesn't mean a party or a picnic as we use it today. Originally it meant "An Appointment." Because of the way it was treated by the Corinthians and on up to the medieval period it later came to mean festival.

    The Feast of the Passover was a holy week!
    It was a week of religious thought.
    It was a week of religious sacrifice.
    It was a week of religious observance.

There was only one day that was observed as Passover Day, but the entire week was a holy week surrounding the Passover Day! The Passover meal that our Lord had with His disciples itself wasn't observed until Tuesday evening of the week. THE LAST SUPPER THAT OUR LORD HAD WITH HIS DISCIPLES WAS NOT THE PASSOVER MEAL! It was the "Early Meal" or the "Preparation Meal", the first meal of the Passover Day. We must stop here and learn that the Jews began their day at 6 o'clock in the evening! Recall that they kept the time as God set it in Genesis1:5 which says, "The evening and the morning were the first day." We keep time today as Gentiles, the way it was instituted during the Roman Era. So the "early meal" of the Passover was taken after 6 o'clock on Tuesday evening. The night was divided into "watches" and the day into hours. Six PM began their new day and lasted 24 hours until six PM the next evening!

(1.) A careful study of Matthew 21 will reveal that on Monday our Lord made His way to Jerusalem. Along the way, He stopped and cursed a fig tree. He went on then to the temple, and cleansed it, overturning the moneychangers' tables, and driving them out! He stopped and taught the people, and received opposition from the Jewish rulers. As evening set in, He went down to Bethany where He was staying. He spent the night there and . . .

(2.) On Tuesday, Jesus went back to Jerusalem, back to the temple, and began teaching parables. Jesus then went to the Mount of Olives. And as it began to get close to Wednesday, probably between 1:30 PM and 2:30 PM, Jesus sent His disciples to prepare for the Passover. And "When the even was come," that is at the beginning of a new day, our Lord went into the upper room and sat down to observe this Supper. The fact that He sat down is a definite indication this was not the Passover meal, for according to Jewish custom (from God's Instruction) the Passover meal was eaten in haste standing up with their loins girt. I say again, this was the "early meal," or the "preparation meal" of the Passover.

I.   This Was Not the First Time This Feast Had Been Observed!

A.   The Jews Had Been Observing the Passover for hundreds of years!

1.   The Passover had it origin in Egypt after Israel had been in bondage 400 years. God said "I will get Me honor in the land tonight. I will pass through the land looking for the blood."

2.   The Passover observance began back in Egypt, and was kept as a memorial of God's great deliverance by the blood of a slain lamb. Each year through

this holy week of observance, the <u>entire nation</u> of Israel was called into remembrance of God's great salvation (deliverance).

3. This miraculous and blessed deliverance (a memorial of salvation) was the greatest thing to have ever happened to Israel. They were memorializing the fact that they were brought out of bondage. Delivered! GLORY! Set free by the blood!

4. Seven feasts (appointments) were held by the chosen nation each year. The Passover was the first one, and all the others connected to it.

II. The Passover Did Not Originate In The Law! (The law came as a result of the Passover)

A. In Exodus 12, God said to Moses concerning the Passover, "This shall be the beginning of months for you!"

B. They were already in the seventh month according to the Jewish calendar, which was the month of <u>Nisan</u>. It's important that the Jewish calendar was very different from ours today. They actually had two calendars: one for governmental purposes, and one for religious purposes.

This first month spoken of in our text was the first month of their religious observances, <u>not governmental</u>.

In the Old Testament, the month of Abib is Chaldaic language, which is the month of Nisan in Hebrew. It is the equivalent to our English month of April. It is known as "the month of new beginnings."

Alfred Edersheim the 17th Century Jewish Rabbi, who was converted to Christianity, became a great author on Jewish tradition. He noted that the thing that concerned him the most was that our preachers today (At that time it was the 17th Century!) had absolutely no idea of <u>Jewish</u> <u>custom</u> and tradition.

Almost all terrible errors made by the expositors and interpreters were due to this misunderstanding.

Let me remind you again that Israel was already in the seventh month of their religious calendar, which was the month of Nisan.

<u>And God Broke in on history and said, "All past history is blotted out as far as you're concerned. This will be your beginning! The seventh month became the first month!</u>

(1.) <u>What a Glorious Doctrine! When Christ breaks in and redemption occurs, the past is blotted out, covered by the blood! And a sin sick sinner has a New Beginning!</u> All your past is history! The day of Salvation is a brand new beginning for you. The Lamb died that the sinner could live!

(2.) God gave more specific instruction on how the Passover was to be carried out.

A, <u>Take a lamb for every household.</u>

B. <u>Put it up for 3 days.</u>

3

C. <u>Slay it. Put the blood in the basin. Take a hyssop branch and dip it in the blood and sprinkle it on the lintels and side posts of the door. Then get behind the door and stay there!</u>

<u>Hyssop</u> – common plant that grew everywhere like ragweed, and is hard to control, like honeysuckle or Kudzu. <u>IT IS A TYPE OF SIN</u>! Before we go further, let's take a look at the basin. Note the spelling – it's not bason, that would mean a bowl, but BASIN. Well, what was a basin and why was it important?

<u>The Basin</u>

In the Egyptian culture in the slave quarters, it was common for their houses to be built with the rear of the houses at the top of a gully that had been dug for the purpose of sanitation. This gully (or deep ditch) ran all the way through the quarters (or at times the village) and into a lagoon or sometimes a river. The front of the house faced the street. All the human waste of the household, feces, urine, table scraps, dirty water, etc. was thrown into that gully. When the torrential rains came, the gully became a raging torrent and washed all the waste and impurities away. (Thus, we have the term "gully-washer.") However, there was another dilemma. Since the houses were built with a dirt floor, built directly on the earth, how were they to keep the water from the rain from running into the house? The problem was solved by digging a shallow ditch to extend around the house with both ends emptying into the gully. The water then would flow around the house and be discharged into the gully. The ditch encircling the house was called "a basin." So not only was the blood applied to the door, not one drop was wasted, it was poured into the basin to surround the house and flow into the area where the stinking, disgusting, foul and repulsive excrement was. Hallelujah!

It doesn't make any difference how vile your sin may be, the blood of Jesus will cover it all, and protect you from the judgment of a righteous God! There is enough blood for the salvation of your entire household!

Then God said, if a household be too small for a lamb, two households can share a lamb. Didn't say if the lamb is too small for the house, but if the household is too small for the lamb!

<u>Christ</u> – (The Lamb) is sufficient for all!

God said I will pass through the land tonight.

I will get me honor tonight. I will visit every household – I will look for the blood. And when I see the blood, I will pass over the door. Thus the name "Passover."

a. <u>Every household was visited</u> from the dungeon, to the slave's quarters, from the common man to the Kings Palace.

Looking for the blood! The Destroyer came looking for the blood!

Jesus said, "I am the door!" Behind the door one is protected by the blood! Praise God, I'm behind the door! CHRIST IS MY SHIELD AND MY DEFENDER! Exodus 12: 24 – 27 "And the Lord said to Moses, 'Each year I want you to keep this as a memorial, an ordinance for thee and thy sons forever!'"

The reason I want you to observe this annually is because I want to give you an opportunity to preach the gospel to your children! For Generations! Jews went by the Lunar Calendar, not the Solar Calendar. The Lunar Calendar is set around the revolution of the moon; as the moon makes its cycle around the earth instead of the earth revolving around the sun. The Solar Calendar that we commonly use today began with Sun Worshipers and Pure Paganism.

The law stated that the Lamb had to be killed in the evening. A point worth mentioning here is that the Moon shines in darkness and the Stars shine in darkness. (Showing God's elect church as a light in a world of darkness.)

The Moon is a reflector of the Sun and we are a reflection of the Son!

We need to note that the Moon cycles each 28 days! In the Lunar Calendar there are four Sabbaths in each month! No fifth Sundays!

The Jews could read the moon and even knew by its size, shape, and location in the sky what time it was! What day and what month as well!

Even today when a woman goes to the doctor and thinks she's pregnant, the doctors figure nine times twenty-eight from the date of conception to tell you when the baby's due.

Sun worshipers began with Nimrod at the Tower of Babel in an act of Rebellion – against God! The Solar Calendar evolved out of Babylon and was popular-ized and fine tuned by the Romans!

Psalm 19:1 "The heavens declare Thy Glory!" meaning the gospel is written in them. They declare the gospel!

A good study can be found on how God works in darkness, but it is only darkness to the world! They slumber and sleep and know nothing of the workings of God!

He hides His work and way from the world and reveals it unto His elect!

The night of the Passover Israel publicly sprinkled the blood.

III. A. They were not ashamed of it!

This was a testimony to the world! The blood was their only hope! They had been in bondage too long to be ashamed!

5

They were ready to do whatever it took – even if it meant being scorned, mocked, and laughed at.

B. <u>God said for them to hold this feast annually, on the same night forever!</u> Well, how were they to know next year when it was the proper day?

C. <u>God said all of you observe it at the same time, on the same day! No matter where you are!</u> They had been slaves! How were they to figure out when to do it? They had no calendar when they came out of Egypt.

D. <u>The moon was their calendar. The Passover was held the week of the first full moon after the first day of spring. How would they know when the first day of spring was?</u> Every Jew knew! It was Jewish Tradition. They knew by the budding of the Almond tree! The Hebrew word for Almond is "shaked" which means "Early Waker." It is the first of the trees to wake from winter sleep!

   a. The almond tree always budded on the first day of spring!

   b. When the almond tree budded, He looked up that night to see when the next full moon was! How were those Jews wondering around in that barren wilderness to know when the almond tree budded? God instructed them to put some certain things in the Ark of the Covenant.

      1. A pot of Manna.

      2. Tablets of stone containing the Law.

      3. Aaron's rod <u>that budded</u>. (Why did it bud? What kind of wood was it made of? – ALMOND!)

So at the time of the next full moon after the budding of the almond tree on Tuesday Evening after 6 PM every Jew all over the land would be celebrating the Passover!

It was a memorial!

And is still a memorial!

E. In the great effort to hide the gospel of God's sovereign grace the devil had to start by "messing up the ordinances of the church" for they speak of the <u>Doctrine of Sovereign Grace</u>!

IV. The Lord's Supper is a picture of Grace!

Note: Christ did not say however often you do this do it in remembrance of me! When are we to have the Lord's Supper?

Somebody said, "Let's have it every fifth Sunday."

Somebody else said, "Oh, twice a year is enough."

Somebody else said, "Let's have it every quarter."

Another one said, "We ought to do it once a month."

And then some said, "We ought to do it every time we meet!"

(There's no Bible for any of this.)

Paul said the Lord's Supper ought to be in order!
Notice, he said, "As oft as ye do this. . . ." You can ask any Jew how oft they celebrate the Passover and they will tell you without hesitation – "ANNUALLY." Well they know how often they do this – Once a year! They had the early meal of the Passover, then they killed a Lamb! They had been doing it annually for hundreds of years.

Paul dealt with some serious problem in the Corinth community regarding the Lord's Supper!

In the Corinthian love feasts they were much abusing the Lord's Supper, eating to the point of gluttony, disregarding the poor, pitching drunks with the wine, but above all else, they did not observe the proper time of day, nor did they kill a lamb! Not only is there a proper day, there's a proper time of day and a proper sacrifice!
The Lamb must be recognized! And the slaughtered Lamb is your only hope! (GET HOLD OF THIS!) The Lord's Supper is about A Slaughtered Lamb! And it was set in order before the law was ever established! It is a memorial to the redemption that is in the Lamb! Every year on the Tuesday Night Before Easter! When is Christmas? December 25. Independence Day? July 4th.
These dates are penned by the Solar Calendar?

Matthew said: As it began to dawn toward the first day of the week.
Mark said: Very early in the morning at the rising of the sun.
Luke said: Very early in the morning.
John said: While it was dark.
(Just before the sun rose. The darkest hour.)

What day of the year is Easter celebrated on? What is the established date of Easter? There's not one!
Man cannot handle this one!
It (The Date) changes every year, because Easter was settled in the creation! It speaks of my Lord and Resurrection!

Now the Babylonians tried to mess it up, by worshipping Ishtar the Sun god. But some of the differences were they waited till the Sun came up! Part of the worship of Ishtar the Sun god was disrobing and lying scantily clad or with no clothes on and basking in the rays of his glory!
Ezekiel 8:14 speaks to us of the Apostate condition of Judah. God called it an abomination.
And Ezekiel said they would set out there with their face toward the Rising Sun and weep for Tamuz, who was supposed to be the miraculous born son of Ishtar and a Babylonish Sun goddess! Ever wonder where the sun rise services came from? The sun has absolutely

nothing to do with the resurrection. The resurrection revolves around the phases of the moon, not the sun. Where does the name Easter come from? From the worship of Ishtar! <u>The Passover had to do with the phase of the moon, not the sun</u>! We need to understand that.

Look at that Lamb! The blood of a Slain lamb! The lamb was slain <u>before the law</u> was ever given!

1. Abraham and Isaac knew about sacrificing lambs. Isaac asked, "Where is the lamb?" Abraham answered, "God will provide Himself a lamb!" Isaac was the Old Testament type of Christ. Abraham saw Christ's day! And rejoiced!
2. What did Noah do when the Ark set down? He offered a sacrifice! A lamb!
3. Abel offered a lamb sacrifice!
4. God Himself in the Garden of Eden offered a lamb!

It's always been a lamb!
The lamb was before the law!
It's always been the blood of the lamb!
For Christ is the lamb!

John the Baptist said about Jesus, "Behold the <u>lamb of God</u>! Who taketh away the sin of the world!"

That night in the Upper Room, Jesus said, "Now boys when you get together each year on the day of the Passover, (on a Tuesday night after 6 o'clock which is the dawning of Wednesday!) do this in remembrance of Me as a memorial. Why? So that when your children ask, "<u>Why do we do this</u>?" You will have opportunity to tell them of Redemption! It's more than Tradition! Jesus said, "Take eat, this is the blood of the New Covenant." He was saying something like this, "Well boys we're going to start something new tonight. From now on when you have this feast, you'll have it in remembrance (or as a memorial) to Me." The Abrahamic covenant became a spiritual type of the covenant of Christ. Which is "all that the father giveth me shall come to me. And he that cometh to me, I will in no wise cast out." (John 6:37)

Do this on the <u>same night every year</u>!
Don't tag it on a picnic, or the close of some Sunday service!
Don't do this haphazardly!
Do it every year, and partake <u>worthily</u>! Not haphazardly!
Note – The Scripture didn't say <u>unworthy</u>, which means undeserving or uncommendable. The word here is <u>unworthily</u>, meaning haphazard, unserious, and unseemly.
I ask is anyone worthy? The Bible says, "No, not one!"

Now I'm not interested in keeping Israel's feast days!
All of the other feasts rested upon the law and the law was fulfilled in Christ. <u>We do not observe them</u>! <u>But the Passover is a memorial</u>. It does not rest upon the law! <u>It rests upon and points to Christ</u>! <u>It's the story of Redemption</u>. It rests upon the blood of the slain Lamb! This is the foundation of our doctrine!
And Paul said – "On the same night our Lord was betrayed!"
<u>The Gospel is established upon this</u>! It's an <u>appointment</u>! It's not a coincidence this supper was held on this night! <u>It wasn't a coincidence Christ and the disciples were there</u>.
It was originally designated by God, for even back then in Egypt God was pointing to His Son, Jesus Christ. He was preparing for us to see it then!
It wasn't a coincidence even where they were in the Upper Room! No! It was an <u>appointment</u>! <u>They planned for it</u>! They knew it was ordained of God!

We plan for Christmas, Thanksgiving, Birthdays, vacations, everything in the world except the thing that is commanded of us in the Scriptures to plan for! The Lord's Supper – The Passover!

If the church is the Pillar and ground of truth, we must seize this opportunity to present the gospel. This God appointed Memorial! A Memorial of Christ – Our Redemption!

Get Hold of This. No excuses are accepted!

In Exodus 34 God said, "Observe this feast and I'll make sure you're protected! Your stuff, your interests, your family, your health!" will have divine protection while you're attending to this the Lord's Business.

That night Judas betrayed Him and the soldiers took Him into custody. At midnight Pilate said, 'Behold, your king!' They had the mock trial that night and hurriedly put Him on the cross. They didn't want Him on the cross on the feast day. (The feast day was a midweek Sabbath [Holy Day] on Thursday) which was Thursday, the feast of Unleavened Bread!

A Word About the Midweek Sabbath:

In our American culture we have sadly mistaken the word "Sabbath" to mean seventh. However, a careful study of the word finds the original Aramaic word "Sabbata" to mean "a day of complete cessation from activity." It also means "a holy day." That leads us to note that the week of the death of our Lord, there was a mid week Sabbath which fell on a Thursday. The Scriptures tell us it was the day of unleavened bread. Therefore Jesus had to be off the cross and in the tomb before 6 PM on Wednesday afternoon, for that was the beginning of the Sabbath, the day of the Feast of Unleavened Bread!

Let's take a quick look, then, at the timeline of events.

On Tuesday evening, a little past 6 o'clock (which was the beginning of their Wednesday) Jesus sat down with the Twelve to have the early meal of the Passover. (We will speak more of this later.) After the "supper," He proceeded to the Garden of Gethsemane.

They had Him on the cross by 9 o'clock Wednesday morning! It generally took 3 days for a person to die on a Roman Cross.

The victims died "inch by inch." But the soldiers went around breaking everybody's legs that year so they would die hurriedly and not be on the cross on the feast day of Unleavened Bread! But when they got to Jesus they said He's already dead. He died in less than six hours!

Why? He knew what time it was! This was the Day of the Sacrifice. He had to be in that tomb by 6 o'clock because that's when the Feast of Unleavened Bread began! He's Sovereignly in control! He died at 3 o'clock on Wednesday (it's also important to note that 3 o'clock was the time of the offering of the evening sacrifice!) Our Lord was off the cross and in the tomb before 6 o'clock on Wednesday!

3 days –

      6 PM Wednesday to 6 PM Thursday
      6 PM Thursday to 6 PM Friday
      6 PM Friday to 6 PM Saturday

(In the tomb on the Sabbath) But as it began to dawn toward the first day of the week.

9

(Six o'clock Saturday Evening began Sunday – The first day of the week.) HE AROSE! Sometime between 6 o'clock Saturday evening and 6 o'clock Sunday morning. Don't pay any attention to this catholic theology of Good Friday. Hogwash! That has to do with Solar Days! You cannot get three days and three nights from Friday to Sunday, no matter how hard you try!

Tuesday Night, the week of the first full moon after 6 o'clock, after the first day of spring is the time to have the Lord's Supper. I believe with all my heart according to all I can find in the Scriptures there is a Day we are supposed to do it. There is a reason we are to do it. There is a purpose in it. And don't think we ought to go about it haphazardly! I think we ought to do it worthily! Seriously!

You've never experienced a blessing in the Lord's Supper like you will experience when it is observed in proper time and order! It's an Appointment! Make your plans now! Don't let anything stop you for on that night, the Tuesday before Easter; the Church should make a statement to the community and to the world about redemption!

The Passover was not based upon the law, but the Lamb!

The most serious business you'll ever get into on this side of eternity is dealing with the Word of God!

The Passover was one of Seven Feasts observed by the Jew throughout their year. All seven of these feasts are given in detail in Leviticus 23. However, the Passover was not under the law. It did not originate in the law. The Passover was observed before the law was ever put in place! The other six were based on the law, and under the law, but not the Passover. Christ fulfilled the law; therefore we do not keep the feasts which were made under the law. But the Passover was put forth for time and eternity for it was based upon the Lamb. GRACE, IF YOU PLEASE!

Now our Lord that night in the Upper Room was telling the disciples that the Lord's Supper was the foundation of the gospel, just as the original Passover was the foundation of the law!

The wall of division between Jew and gentile had been torn down in Christ! And the Lord's Supper was now the New Testament sealed in His blood! And Christ said as oft as ye do this, do it in remembrance of me! "From now on I am the Lamb!" The Passover was held annually as a memorial, so that when your children shall ask "what mean ye by this service?" you could point back to the Lamb and tell them of redemption!

The risen Christ was the Lamb slain from the foundation of the world, because God knew from the foundation of the world He was going to be saving some people!

When Christ said "I have a Baptism to be baptized with," He was speaking of the wrath of God on Calvary. He would be submerged in God's wrath! Our physical Baptism pictures – the wrath of God poured out on Christ, He bore it and then was resurrected!

In Egypt, the destroyer was speaking of God's judgment. The judgment of God was going to visit every household. God's judgment is coming to your household. The only thing that saved Israel was the application of blood. On Calvary the destroyer came again and visited Christ. The judgment of God was poured out upon Him, but He bore it for the sins of His people. Because they couldn't come to God without a sacrifice that had been slaughtered! Christ became the sin and the sacrifice on Calvary!

Salvation is not a sinner coming to God – it is God coming to the sinner!
Moses didn't give an invitation, He gave a command! "KILL A LAMB AND SPRINKLE ITS BLOOD!"

The story of redemption centers upon the Lamb.

The gospel centers upon the Lamb! Thank God I have a lamb! Christ Jesus, my Lord!

In Church services I have often said, "Raise your hand if you think there's anything about your life that God will accept! If not, you need a Lamb!"

"If you don't believe you're going to hell because you're a guilty sinner, you don't need a Lamb, and you don't need a Savior, but if you do you need a lamb!"

Romans 3 says there's none good, no not one. There is none that doeth good. Then how will we escape damnation? We must have a Lamb!

In Egypt they couldn't plan their own Salvation. God had to plan it.

They couldn't save themselves, God had to save them!

The command was given to Israel only! Slay a lamb! Sprinkle the blood of the lamb.

Then they had to get behind the door and stay there hidden behind the door. In the New Testament Christ said, "I am the door!" We must be hidden behind Him!

We enter in through Him and are hidden behind Him, therefore, we are eternally protected, eternally safe, and eternally secure!

Chapter 2

When Do We Have the Supper?

1 Corinthians 11:23-27
Exodus 12
Matthew 26:18-29

Preachers: Bring people to this Book!
Stand in the Truth if you have to stand alone!

Our Lord rose from the dead after 6 o'clock on Saturday evening, which was the beginning of the first day of the week for the Jew. Remember their days began at 6 PM and ended at 6 PM the next day. The Scripture says that Christ arose as it began to dawn toward the first day of the week. Now this particular day was the ending of Sabbath. Mary, Peter, and John waited until the Sabbath was ended before they visited the tomb. To do so earlier would have been a desecration of the Sabbath. This is also the reason it was dark, and they needed to carry a torch. This also explains why, when Jesus began to talk to Mary, she supposed it to be the gardener. It was dark and she couldn't see who it was that was addressing her.

The story in the Scripture we have read opens up on Tuesday evening, after 6 o'clock and was the early meal, or preparation meal of the Passover. Therefore this was the beginning of Wednesday. Remember the Jews operated on a lunar month rather than a solar month. This was Passover week, and all the Jews all over the land were keeping this appointment. They had been keeping it for hundreds of years. This observance began hundreds of years ago when God delivered His people from bondage by the blood of the Lamb. This story is found in Exodus, chapter 12.

This deliverance was the greatest thing to ever happen to Israel! And God commanded that it be kept as a memorial unto Him, every year, forever! He went on and added that "when your children shall ask about it, you would be able to tell them of God's redemption through the blood of the Lamb."

If you don't understand the Passover, you won't understand why there is an observance of the Lord's Supper on an annual basis. Our Lord said "as oft as ye do this," and they knew exactly what He was talking about, for they had been doing it every year since their deliverance from Egypt. They didn't do it every fifth Sunday, or once a quarter, they did it annually as the Lord commanded! They would not have heard of doing it any other time, for that would have been a desecration of the Lord's commandment! Now remember, in just a few days from this time, the Holy Ghost would visit them on the Day of Pentecost (another feast, or appointment) and the church would be birthed in mighty power. The early church continued keeping the Passover annually just as God commanded, only now, for the church, they no longer had to slaughter a lamb, but rather commemorated the Lamb who was slaughtered! They partook of the body and blood of Him who redeemed them in a memorial called the Lord's Supper! When Christ said "this is the New Covenant in my blood, He was telling them He was fulfilling the Old Covenant and making a <u>New One</u>. Every year up until this time they had to slaughter a lamb, but no longer would they slaughter a lamb, <u>from now on He was their lamb</u>, slaughtered, sacrificed, offered, and accepted by God. From now on they would look back to Him! This is the <u>New Testament</u>. The word testament simply means "covenant."

Some of the great truths of the Passover are that:

1. SALVATION IS THE WORK OF GOD ALONE!
2. People can only be saved by redemption.
3. God did not say to them, "If you'll just come on out of Egypt, or come on over to Canaan and I'll save you." No! He didn't say, "Come on over to where I am."
4. <u>He went to where they were</u>, for they could not go to Him!
5. They weren't redeemed by keeping the commandments, for the commandments had not yet been given.
6. Their Salvation was a Sovereign act of God alone, and depended on God's absolute Sovereignty! It was an act of a sovereign, holy, righteous, merciful God!
7. In Egypt Israel was beyond self help! They were totally and completely in bondage, slaves to the Egyptians, and could not break loose, could not save themselves! Notice the Scripture says, "And the Word of the Lord <u>came unto Moses</u>." "And the Lord said . . . (to Moses), <u>Salvation is a Sovereign Act of God</u>! – That's how Redemption comes <u>God must speak first</u>!
8. <u>They did not "step out by faith and claim God's promise" until first God claimed them</u> and gave them the deliverance necessary to be able to "step out and claim His promises." <u>The Word of God must come to you</u>! Have you ever experienced that?
9. He had to first make it possible by setting them free! "Faith cometh by hearing . . . ." God had to speak faith unto them in order for them to follow and obey Him.

It is important for us to understand that life begins when God speaks! That was set in order in the creation. It's a picture of Salvation. God speaks, life comes; God speaks, miracles happen!

In Exodus 12 God said this shall be the beginning of months for you!

1. Everything that happened to you before now is deadness – GOD BLOTTED OUT THE PAST!
2. Therefore their deliverance began with an act of God, in fact, it began in God! It was in what He did, not what they could do!
3. The history of the unbeliever is death once Christ comes to him! You may remember when you were saved, and you can look back at that time and place and rejoicingly say, "RIGHT THERE IS WHERE IT ALL BEGAN!" Everything before that time is deadness. Life began when God spoke!
   In the Old Testament – From the creation, life began at the Word of God!
   In the New Testament – The dead rose when Jesus spoke, In Salvation; life begins at the Word of God! No wonder the Scripture says, "<u>in the beginning was the Word, and the Word was with God, and the Word was God</u>." Hallelujah! His Word is life for He is life!

The whole of Redemption centers upon a lamb!
YOU CANNOT APPROACH GOD APART FROM A LAMB!

It's the lamb all the way through the Bible!

There's no hope for any man apart from the blood of the lamb!

> God said to Moses, "speak to the children of Israel and tell them they are to take a lamb and kill it, and sprinkle its blood on the lintels and side posts of the door! Pour the blood in the basin and get behind the door!

1. In Genesis a lamb was slain in the Garden of Eden for Adam.
2. Abel slaughtered a lamb.
3. Abraham and Isaac spoke of the lamb for a sacrifice.
4. In Exodus it was a lamb for each family.
5. In Leviticus upon setting up the priesthood, a lamb was to be slain for them, for their redemption!

Glory to God, there was a day appointed when a lamb was to be slain for ME! MY LAMB WAS SLAIN! MY LAMB WAS AN ACCEPTABLE SACRFICE! PERFECT, SPOTLESS – ACCEPTABLE TO GOD!

> Who killed the Lamb?
> Note: Thousands of lambs were killed the night of the first Passover, and thousands of lambs were killed annually thereafter.
> But notice: God always speaks of it in the singular. As though they were all one lamb, God was talking about "a lamb," singular. Why? All those lambs represented one lamb – because God was looking at Christ! His Son dying on Calvary!
> They would cut the throat of that little lamb and pour its blood into a basin, or on an altar. But God was looking at the blood of His Son! On Calvary! As though it was His blood being poured upon the altar and sprinkled upon the Mercy Seat.
>
> God looked at the whole mass of lambs as ONE Lamb!
>
> There is only one lamb in God's Book! And that's Christ!
>
> When the Scripture says Christ was the "firstborn among many brethren" Romans 8:29, it is pointing to this night here in Egypt!
> What happened to the firstborn where there was no slain lamb?
> He was destroyed by the destroyer!
> What happened to Christ?
> He was destroyed of the destroyer! He suffered the wrath and judgment of God!
> What was Calvary about? Slaughtering the Lamb!
>
> An offended God poured out His wrath upon the Lamb. God slaughtered Him on Calvary! The wrath of God was exhausted! Poured upon Him until there was none left.
> God said when I see the blood, I will pass over the door and not suffer the destroyer to come in.

A. The destroyer came to destroy, to bring judgment. He would have had no respect for the blood of the lamb!
BUT GOD DID! For He was looking at His Son!
It was either the lamb was to die – OR THE FIRSTBORN WAS TO DIE – But one or the other must be slain to appease God!
CHRIST WAS THE FIRSTBORN AND THE LAMB!

That night in Egypt –
God came looking for the blood!
  a. But what if a thief was behind that door?
   God was looking for the blood of a Lamb.
  b. But what if a drunkard was behind that door?
   What if a harlot, a prostitute, was behind the door?
   What if a drug addict was behind the door?
   What if a gambler was behind the door?
   God was looking for the blood of the Lamb!
   And all who trusted the blood of the Lamb were saved!

Bring all the howling accusations you want, but when a man or a woman trusts the blood of the Lamb, "who can lay anything against the charge of God's elect?"
The past has been blotted out! God said shed the blood then get behind the door – and when He passed over the door all were safe who were behind Him. Jesus said, "I am the Door!" Satan would have to come through Him to get to ME! Can you not see how secure I am? He's my firstborn, my Lamb, my Door!

The Lamb was killed as a substitute. If you don't believe that, you'll suffer the wrath of the offended God.

Redemption was not based on anything they did. Their redemption rested in the lamb, which was a substitutionary death. It was either the lamb or the firstborn. Christ was both the lamb and the firstborn!

We are secured absolutely, redeemed totally and completely by the death of our substitute, Jesus Christ!
And He was the Sacrifice, the Lamb slain from the foundation of the world.
Lastly, we can only have peace with God through an accomplished redemption.
He said, "IT IS FINISHED!"

If you are going to shout, shout over the merits of the cross! Over absolute, complete, finished Redemption! If He got you in, He'll take you through. He that hath begun a good work in you will perform it!

The Scripture says, ". . . for the joy that was set before Him." Hebrews 12:2
"He endured the cross. . ."

Christ rejoiced (!) in His work!
But why would Christ rejoice if Salvation and Redemption depended on you, what you could, would, or wouldn't do? For then Salvation would rest

in you!

Redemption then would not be complete, for Christ would have to wait to see what you would do. It would all be finished except your part! Therefore it would really be unfinished. How could He rejoice in an unfinished work? Something had to be done to keep God from putting you in Hell because of your sin. And it did not rest in you! It rested in a Lamb!

If our Lord accomplished only as much as some folks think, how could He have any joy about Calvary?

But it is finished! Redemption is in the Lamb.

He is the Author: The Lamb slain from the foundation of the world.

He is the Finisher: John said, "I heard the voice of a lion and turned and saw a Lamb. He also saw a number no man could number crying, 'WORTHY IS THE LAMB!'"

Now Christ is to the church, what the lamb was to the Jew! – OUR SACRIFICE!

From that night our Lord met with the disciples in the Upper Room, and said this is a New Covenant, we no longer slay a lamb – WE BEHOLD THE LAMB!

And are partakers of His body and blood every year in an eternal memorial to Him.

FOR WHEN OUR CHILDREN ASK WHY? WHY THIS WAY, WHY THIS TIME, WHY THIS DAY – WE MAY SPEAK TO THEM OF REDEMPTION!

Christ can be seen in the annual observation of the Lord's Supper.

We that are redeemed in the family of God can look both ways in time. We can look backward into history, and if our churches hadn't gotten into such a haphazard manner of observing the Lord's Supper, we could look at the annual observation of the Lord's Supper and see Christ. Next, we could look on back farther and pick up on the Passover and see Christ. And then on back beyond that to the sacrificial lamb of Abraham and Isaac, of Noah, of Abel, of God in the Garden of Eden – and see Christ.

And then look into the future and see the church carrying this on annually and then see the coming of the Lord. Then, seeing the blood-washed crowd around the throne of God saying, "Worthy is the Lamb that was slain from the foundation of the world!" He is Worthy! He is Worthy, Hallelujah! It's always been the Lamb! Christ the Lamb – AND THE LAMB SITS UPON THE THRONE!

I Corinthians 11:23-24
Exodus 12:21-27

Calvary was no accident. Christ was the Lamb slain. He is Lord of Lords, King of Kings, Ruler, Counselor, Controller, The Fairest of Ten Thousand, He is Sovereign. He is Worthy!

Isaiah 64:6

Let's now reiterate the Events of the Passover Feast.

IT WAS A WEEK LONG CELEBRATION
1. On Tuesday evening a little after 6 PM, our Lord sat down with the Twelve to have the early meal.

2. On Wednesday they had Him on the cross by 9 AM.
3. At noon a darkness settled upon the scene that blotted out the noon day sun for the space of 3 hours.
4. He died at 3 PM (The same time of the evening sacrifice.)
5. They took Him off of the cross and had Him in the grave by 6 PM so as not to desecrate themselves for the Feast of Unleavened Bread which began at 6 PM on Wednesday evening. (The beginning of Thursday, the midweek Sabbath.)
6. He was in the grave on the weekly Sabbath (which was Saturday) and got up some-time after 6 PM on Saturday evening. And when they came very early in the morning on Sunday, He was arisen from the grave!

Chapter 3

With Christ in the Garden

Isaiah 53:4-7; 10-11
Matthew 26:36-46
Hebrews 5:7-9

In Hebrews Chapter 5 we go with Christ into the Garden. The Scripture declares that it was there we find Him in the "Days of His Flesh! Flesh means "weakness." Gethsemane was considered to be the place of His "flesh" or "weakness."

The thing that bothers me most in our churches today, is that our people know so little about the events surrounding our Lord at Calvary, and the great price He paid for our redemption. We speak of it so frivolously. It appears to me we have not yet understood that the plan and purpose of redemption was set in order before the foundation of the world, and Christ was dying to save a people! When I think of the events surrounding Calvary, of Gethsemane, and the mock trial, of the spittle and the blood, and the dying of Our Lord, I almost want to take my shoes off when I even meditate on it, for <u>this is the holiest ground of all</u>! <u>THIS IS THE HOLY OF HOLIES FOR THE CHURCH</u>!

When the supper had finished, Jesus and the eleven (Judas had already gone to make his deal to sell our Lord for the price of a slave) went out to the Garden of Gethsemane. There were multitudes of the followers of Jesus who were already in their own homes, not realizing what was occurring to Our Lord that night. Even the eleven with Him did not understand what was happening. Of these 11, He left eight of them just outside the garden gate and He took Peter, James, and John with Him on further down into the garden. He said to them, "You wait here and watch and pray while I go yonder and pray." He didn't pray with them, He prayed alone that night. It had come the time when our Lord must tread the winepress of God's wrath, and He must do it alone. The heart of our Savior was heavy with sorrow and grief and unutterable woe as He knelt there that night in the garden. For 4 days before this occurrence, it is recorded by John that Jesus said, "Now is my soul troubled." (John 12:27) Matthew said, "He began to be sorrowful and very heavy." (Matthew 26:37) "Very heavy" means "so grieved so as to be distracted from those around Him." He went on to say, "My soul is exceeding sorrowful, even unto death." Have you ever been under so much pressure, and so absorbed in your mind over that which was troubling you that you didn't even pay attention to people talking to you? Or people had to speak to you two or three times to get your attention? That's how our Lord was! Mark said, "He was sore amazed and very heavy." (or in great agony) The best reference I could get on this was in Hebrews 12:21 which speaks of Moses when he stood in the presence of the Lord on Mt. Sinai and "did exceedingly fear and did quake (tremble)." Our Lord was in great agony. The word <u>Agony</u> means, "a mental and emotional pressure and stress so tremendous, that it causes a writhing, a turning and twisting; a pacing, accompanied with great pain." Have you ever seen a man bend over with pain? This was our Lord that night in the garden. Oh, it breaks my heart when I realize the agony of Our Lord. It's hard to understand, that Christ bore such pressure and agony. I know He knew this is what He came into this world to do, but as that hour approached, and the grief of that hour drew near, He began to fully comprehend in His flesh the meaning of SIN! It was approaching time now that He was to take His official position in regard to the sin of the world. That hour was approaching when He was to be made SIN! When the Lord was to lay upon Him the iniquity of us all, and the chastisement of our peace He was to bear! The hour had come, He was the sin bearer and yet more, He was the substitute for our sin, and yet more, and as He approached this hour in Gethsemane, He did fear, and quake, was grief stricken and exceedingly sorrowful and in great agony as the view of shame and suffering, and the very departure of His Father came closer upon Him! There's nothing more terrifying than to feel like God has left you alone! Oh, the desperation of that feeling of anguish! The helplessness of such an hour!

Our Lord had to become helpless into the very hands of sinners! So helpless was He that He was like a lamb! being led to the slaughter! As a lamb! NO DEFENSE! AS A LAMB! SPEAKING NOT A WORD! AS A LAMB! HELPLESS! HUMBLE! BENDING HIS BACK TO THE SMITERS! As the hour of helplessness approached Him, He was tempted in all points like as we are, yet He had nothing to do with Sin! The word tempted means "TRIED," and yet it had nothing to do with SIN! How Can That Be? He had already said in John 14:30 "The Prince of this world cometh …." But he hath nothing in me. [There is no sin in me.] He is coming; Satan is coming! Why? This was a showdown! In Luke 22:53, when that crowd came to carry him to Pilate's Hall, He said, "This is your hour, and the (hour of) the power of darkness! Satan Did Come! with all His power and all His strength, He had come! CHRIST OUR LORD was no stranger to Satan. Way back before the calling of this earth out of its murky waters of darkness, iniquity was found in Lucifer, Son of the morning, He was cast out of heaven with one third of the very angels of Heaven following Him! He became the Prince of the power of the air. He was no longer the son of the morning, but now the Prince of darkness! His evil presence on this earth created such havoc that the judgment of God was called upon it, and in Genesis 1:2 due to the efforts of Satan we will find the earth formless and void under the judging of God! When Adam and Eve were placed in the garden, Satan was already there, to attempt to thwart the sovereign plan of God, and stop the destiny of God's judgment upon him! From that point on, there is a running battle between Christ and Satan throughout the pages of the Scripture until we come to Calvary. AND HERE IS THE ULTIMATE SHOWDOWN!

In the wilderness our Lord had overcome him, but now here he is once again in the garden! But this time, it's another garden, and it's not Adam, it's Christ!

Oh, here comes the Prince of this world with all his power and all his forces.

Think about it. The great agony of our Lord! Mental stress, so great that it's unbearable, emotional stress so great that it's unbearable, pressure so great, so unbearable that it causes writhing and twisting and pacing and turning. Why? Because of the attack of Satan! Can't you hear Satan saying, "No one is following you now! Where are the multitudes you fed, and the great crowds you preached to? No one believes you or believes in you! Your closest companions are sleeping; they're not even concerned with you! They won't even sit with you one hour while you're in agony!"

Do you remember how our Lord paced back and forth that night? He would pace back and forth from His place of prayer and agony to the place where He left the disciples. And He'd find them sleeping, and wake them up and say, "What, could ye not watch with me one hour?" The word watch means, "as a comforter would sit with a sick friend."

That night in the garden, as Satan began his attack, the Son of Man had "NO COMFORTERS!"

And Satan would go on, "Oh, you Solitary One, Look at My Dominance! I am the ruler and controller of this world! People do not care for you! They are interested in the things I can give them! They are looking for pleasures, and popularity, and money, and power! Why just an hour of their time is too much to ask! In fact, you ask way too much of their lives! You want them to change too much! And they're not interested! I rule them, I control them, AND ALL YOU WOULD DO FOR THEM IS IN VAIN!"

And just as the angelic host of heaven came and announced the birth of our Lord, all the demonic host of the legions of darkness attacked Him at His death, and it began in Gethsemane! Can you not see our Lord writhing and trembling and quaking as the myriads of demons circle about Him, hurling their onslaughts!?

"Where is God to help You in this war? You are forsaken, and even Your closest companions don't care about the pressure You're under!

And look at You, in all Your grief and sorrow, trembling, and quaking. And then You want to tell me You're the Lion of the tribe of Judah! You're a weakling! You're not at all who You say You are!" Can you imagine the onslaughts of Satan that night!?

Forsaken of God! And smitten, treading the winepress of God's wrath! (Isaiah said He tread it alone!)

Can you not hear Satan saying to the Son of Man, "Why you cannot redeem these people! Being forsaken of God has rendered you helpless before me! AND YOU WILL SEE WHAT I WILL DO WITH YOU! I WILL DESTROY YOU!"

Three times our Lord went and viewed His disciples, His closest companions (Peter, James, and John). And during the greatest ordeal to date in His earthly life, THEY ARE ASLEEP!

But Hebrews chapter 12:4 infers to us that "He resisted even unto blood" that onslaught of Satan! He prayed, and was heard, and He prayed the more earnestly! He prayed until His sweat became as great drops of blood falling to the ground! Hebrews 5:7 calls it the "days of His flesh" that is, "the days of His utter weakness," and says, "He lifted up prayers of supplication with strong cryings and tears" AND WAS HEARD!

PRAYER IS ASKING FOR SOMETHING TO BE GIVEN.

SUPPLICATION IS ASKING FOR SOMETHING TO BE DONE!

Our Lord was praying for something to be given and something to be done, and was pouring His heart out in the face of Satan!

I don't believe that any creature suffered like our Savior suffered! Oh, the Agony our Lord suffered that night in the garden! Shrieking, and crying, and trembling, moaning, staggering and falling, twisting, and writhing.

Our Lord was under such pressure, such mental and emotional anguish, such an onslaught of Satan THAT HE WOULD WELCOME DEATH! The death on the cross was a welcome sight to Him!

During this onslaught of Satan, notice the conduct of our Lord. Luke 22:44 "And being in agony He prayed more earnestly . . . ."

He prayed! The more Satan attacked Him, the more earnestly did our Lord pray!
He prayed alone.
Family prayer is good, praying in church is good, but that prayer to God alone in the secret place is what really gets the job done!
He didn't wait until He was suffering the onslaught of Satan to pray.
He prayed alone often.
He prayed in the mountains.
He prayed in solitary places.
He spent nights in prayer. He was acquainted with secret praying! That's how He knew it would work that night in Gethsemane, because it had already worked for Him before! One of the first things I learned, even before I was saved, and especially after I was saved, was to pray!

My daddy first taught me to pray. Some of the old time preachers and deacons then continued teaching me to pray! As a young lad, they would take me with them to pray! We'd meet on the side of the mountain and pray. Sometimes till the wee hours of the morning! Those men would make special efforts TO PRAY! Society doesn't know about this kind of praying today. They taught us young men and boys TO PRAY! Prayer is not only the key to unlock the gates of heaven, but is also the key to lock the gates of hell!

Christ Prayed Humbly! Luke said He knelt in prayer. Matthew said He fell on His face! He humbled Himself before God! Kneeling is an act of humbleness and submission! To fall on your face is to be so humbled as to consider yourself as a worm, or as the dust of the ground. It is an act of absolute yieldedness. It is the mark of a great burden too heavy to bear up under! It is to say I cannot go further without divine intervention! Divine help!

And He prayed as a little child.

He said, "Oh my Father." The cry of a child in fear, hurt, and desperation.

He prayed, Abba, Father. The cry of a baby. A helpless baby! This was no pretence, no show, as we sometimes pray in pretended humbleness. His grief was of vast distress. He was broken in anguish, and in great agony, and being attacked by Satan. His access to God was to come in humbleness and as a helpless baby! It was a father – child relationship! It's God's will to suffer little children to come unto Him. And God will hear the cries of His children! You cannot come to God on the strength of your position, YOU MUST COME TO HIM AS A CHILD!

It was a Persevering Prayer!

He kept praying the same prayer over and over! The prayer of Jesus Christ in the Garden is in the imperfect tense, indicating it was repetitive. He prayed over and over until He was heard!

It was a Prayer of Resignation.

He resigned Himself to the will of the Father. (Not as I will but as Thy will.)

What a blessed day when we learn Prayer is not to change God's mind, but to RESIGN YOURSELF TO THE WILL OF GOD!

He yielded to what God was doing!

Look again at Hebrews 5:7. He offered up prayers and supplication with strong cryings and tears, meaning "hysterical screams and floods of tears."

Can you imagine that? Our Lord there in Gethsemane that night in hysterical screams and floods of tears! OH, THIS WAS THE DAY OF HIS WEAKNESS! Where did these hysterical screams and floods of tears come from? The Bible said He feared! Now that's hard for me to grasp. Our Lord took on pure manhood that night becoming weak and facing Satan in that hour of utter weakness! He bore the emotions of manhood. And from those emotions came hysterical screams and floods of tears!

But that very verse goes on to say AND HE WAS HEARD! He lifted up His cries and prayers to Him who was able to deliver Him AND WAS HEARD!

Now let's look at another meaning of this cup. He was praying, "Let this cup pass from Me!" And He was heard!

First, the cup was the fourth cup. The cup of benediction. He was praying His way to Calvary!

Secondly, it was a cup of tears! A cup of fear and trembling and quaking! A cup of hysterical agony and floods of tears.

But the Scripture says He was heard. And God sent an angel to strengthen Him!

Oh, what a blessed hour when you pray till the strength comes and you have victory in the power of the Holy Ghost! Victory to face Satan's onslaughts, victory to fight he battle, victory to keep on keepin' on!

Look at Him now. See the strength of His character! The strengthening has come!

Jesus walks up to His disciples and said, "Sleep on now, take your rest."

Judas walks up and Jesus says to him, "Friend, wherefore art thou come?"

Such a <u>calmness</u> and a <u>dignity</u> of glory about Him.

A few minutes ago He was writhing and screaming with hysterical screams. He was pacing and praying. He looked like a wild man.

But see Him now. So calm. He wasn't praying to get out of the cross. He was praying for God to be glorified in giving Him an attitude of calmness in the midst of His trial that would show forth that Glory!

Now watch Him. After the strengthening, He prayed the more earnestly. Was Satan still around? Sure He was! Was He still hurling onslaughts and putting on pressure? Sure, <u>but now our Lord was strengthened! The cup had passed. And now for the joy that was set before Him, He was about to take that journey to Calvary's Hill.</u>

As our Lord now was praying more earnestly, Satan hurled another attack. I can hear Him say, "They'll kill you, and you don't want to shed your blood."

And His sweat suddenly became as great drops of blood just to show Satan how freely He could AND <u>WOULD</u> shed His blood! He <u>gave</u> His blood!

Sudden fear, sudden alarm, or sudden terrifying, will cause people to faint. Now what brings about that fainting is that all the blood in the head drains and it doesn't get the right amount of circulation to the brain and all the blood of the body rushes inward toward the heart to nourish the inner man. And that sudden draining of blood from the brain causes a temporary unconsciousness!

But Not our Lord.

"Satan, at this point in all of my weakness, I want to show you how freely my blood will flow!" And of His own will, His blood came forth and fell to the ground! Neither man nor Satan took His blood; He shed it freely to become our ultimate sacrifice for Sin!

Notice the peace He has now! How calm He is! How dignified He is! He had been heard! AND THIS IS HOW YOU'LL KNOW YOU'VE BEEN HEARD, AND STRENGTHENED! When God gives you the victory, it will change your attitude over the same circumstance. You'll have peace and dignity.

Notice now His glorified dignity and calmness as Judas comes to Him. He says very calmly, "Wherefore art thou come friend?"

Judas had already told those to whom he had betrayed Jesus, "You'll know Him, because it will be He whom I kiss." And Jesus said, "Judas! Betrayest thou the Son of Man with a kiss?"

They came running up to lay hold on Jesus and Peter took his sword and swung it at Malchus, the nephew of the High Priest. And as Malchus ducked, Peter's sword clipped his ear and cut it off.

Just a few minutes ago, when our Lord was depressed and full of fear and so hysterical in His robes of manhood, He would have probably yelled, "Kill them all!" But not now, He had been heard and strengthened.

Now He said, "Peter, put away your sword," and very calmly He picked up that ear and <u>performed a miracle right there</u> by putting it back on!

They said, "We're looking for Jesus," and with a quiet dignity He answered, "<u>I am He</u>." And the Bible said that they fell backward to the ground. What Glory! and Power. The weakness of His flesh was gone! Oh, the glory that was set before Him to endure the cross!

Look at His calmness that night when Herod would speak to Him, and He wouldn't even answer!

The authorities said, "We have the power to save your life or put you to death." He said, "You don't have that power, the only power you have is what God gives to you. And if He didn't want this to happen you couldn't do this to Me!"

There were certain benefits divined from the agony of our Lord that night in the garden. A part of the work of our Lord was accomplished <u>that Night</u> that has to do with our Salvation! This is the place, the time, and point where He became the Author of our Salvation! He had already shed His blood; therefore He could boldly say to that thief, "This day thou shalt be with Me in Paradise!"

In Gethsemane our Lord became helpless, and Paul, in Acts 8:33, says His judgment or "Authority" was taken away. He suffered fleshly manhood against an onslaught of Satan like no man had ever suffered that Night in Gethsemane! And His authority was taken away! His authority, His ability as the Son of God, His judgment was taken away! and He became help-less! A Lamb being led to the slaughter!

He was more than just a martyr. Millions of men died down through the ages, a martyr's death, but who are they? What did they accomplish? They are for the most part forgotten! Well where are they now? Their bodies remain in the grave! But what about Christ, wasn't His authority taken away? Yes. But it was given to Him again in the strengthening! Now He could say "all power is given unto Me in heaven and earth." And in that power and authority our Lord burst forth from the grave in the dynamism of His resurrection! He is Lord! Sovereign Lord! He hath redeemed us and we can know Him in the fellowship of His suffering! For He suffered Absolute Manhood against the onslaught of Hell, beginning that night in Gethsemane! But God gave Him power and dignity to bear up under all that hell could put on Him, and all the wrath of God that was poured out on Him!

Did Satan stop then? Oh no, Gethsemane was just the beginning!

But now our Lord had suffered as a man the onslaught of Satan, and defeated Him in this point!

And remember those two all important words – "In Him." The Scripture says that, "We might be made the righteousness of God IN HIM." No wonder He could say, "That where I am there ye may be also." HE IS LORD! Hebrews 5:7-9 says He was made "perfect." That word perfect means "the fulfillment of its purpose."

In other words it says, "And having fulfilled His purpose through suffering." His purpose could not have been fulfilled had He not suffered the intense agony of Gethsemane.

Hebrews 2:17-18 says, "He was made like unto His brethren to "succor" them. "Succor" means to relieve, to help, to deliver, to draw near.

He is Lord!
Do you need relief tonight?
Are you grieved and worried?
Do you fear and tremble and wonder how you're gonna make it through?
Do you cry and wring your hands and pace back and forth with worry and fear over some matter or some situation in your life?
Come to Him. He knows how you feel!
The situation might not be moved, but He will give you peace and power and provision to make it through!

Just whisper to Him . . .
Oh, Lamb of God I come!

Chapter 4

The Suffering Savior

Isaiah 53:3
John 13:31-38

We must understand that we cannot separate the death of our Lord on Calvary from His life. Most folks think that Jesus just passed through for a few years preaching some good sermons, but that didn't account for too much; that all that really counted was His death on the cross. But that is a grave mistake. If Christ our Lord had not lived a perfect, spotless, sinless life, His blood could not have atoned for our sin. If He had not lived a life fulfilling the law, and the prophets, His death could not have paid our debt! Death is the climax of suffering, it is not the suffering itself, but our Lord suffered. He <u>had</u> to suffer to fulfill the Scripture, "for by His stripes we are healed." "He was oppressed, He was afflicted, "but as a lamb being led to the slaughter, said not a word." Satan attacked Him full force in the garden of Gethsemane, and our Lord prayed with hysterical cries and floods of tears and was heard. And strengthened by the Angel sent from God.

Being then led away from the garden as a captive, He was taken to a mock trial. The Sanhedrin had a court and the Jews tried him, they sent Him over to Pilate, who tried Him, and sent Him over to Herod. Herod tried Him and sent Him back to Pilate. And all this time, the bloodthirsty multitude was screaming and raving in the street.

Now I have already stated to you that when it comes to the agony, and suffering and death of our Lord, and the events surrounding Calvary, we are treading on Holy Ground! WE ARE MUCH TOO CASUAL, TOO HAPHAZARD AND "HO-HUM" WHEN WE SPEAK OF CALVARY IN THIS MODERN AGE! But friends, this for the church is, THE HOLY OF HOLIES!

Calvary is the place where our High Priest entered and the blood was poured out! So holy is the ground I feel like taking my shoes off when I speak of it! When you think about our Lord, and how He became sin for us, and consumed the fury of the wrath of God, and suffered all the powers of hell for us, it will make you want to take your shoes off! Oh, if it ever dawns on you what our Lord suffered, you can't help but want to take your shoes off on such holy ground!

This thing of being a Christian has nothing to do with having your name on a church roll, or shaking a preacher's hand, or even being baptized. IT HAS TO DO WITH HIM! OUR SALVATION HAS TO DO TOTALLY WITH HIM! He instigated our salvation, planned it before the foundation of the world, and in the fullness of time, came into this world. <u>God</u> manifest in the flesh. <u>He came at the right time; He came at the right place; He came through the right family, was baptized at the right place, began His ministry at the right place, preached the right sermons, performed the right miracles, everything about our Lord was exactly right!</u> The Scripture, the law, and the prophets were all fulfilled in Him! <u>There has never been a time when He was out of control</u>! He is absolutely totally sovereign! He came into this body of flesh and His entire life operated according to a divine plan! Nothing about it was in error, nor by chance or accident but it was all <u>on purpose</u> for the redemption of an elect bride – His church! And thank God I'm in it! And nothing about my Salvation (even my life) has been by accident. I was born on time, in the right year, to right parents, had the right experiences in life as designed just for me. Been to the right churches, heard the right preachers, and called to salvation right on time! I'm where I am now by the design of God!

In John 13:31-38 it seemed that Peter was bragging, but at that time, Peter really felt like He was willing to lay his life down for Jesus. Look what Jesus said,
"Wilt thou lay down thy life for my sake? Verily, verily, I say unto thee, the cock shall not crow until thou hast denied me thrice."

Aren't you glad that our Lord knew exactly what we were going to do, before He even saved us!? He knew how you and I would react under every circumstance. And He saved us anyway! Knowing full well that Peter was going to be the man who would deny Him 3 times in the very night that He Himself was to be crucified, and yet He called Peter THE ROCK!

The Lord knew everything you were going to do before He saved you! When Christ went to the cross all of your sins were yet future. He knew everything you would do. And even what you were capable of doing; He knew how you would react under every circumstance – AND HE SAVED YOU ANYWAY!

What about a love like that! Love is seen by its deeds! In fact our Lord said, "Let us not love in word or in tongue but in deeds." Your salvation is the deed of God's love! Calvary is the deed of God's love! Love is seen best in its kindness after it has been made to suffer! And the suffering of Christ shows His "great love wherewith He loved us . . . ."

"Love covereth a multitude of sins." That's how Christ could know what you were going to do, how you were going to react, how you would treat Him, and save you anyway! His love covered your sins! Oh, if only we could learn to love like that! We can only have that kind of love through Christ! If we want to have that kind of love, we need to get more of God, for God is love!

You see a young man, he may be a rascal, a reprobate, a deadbeat, he drinks a lot, and drives recklessly. He's in and out of trouble, and the whole county knows it. But you go talk to that boy's mama. She'll never ever mention the bad things about him. And she'll tell you so many good things about him, you'll wonder if you're talking about the same boy. She'll act like she doesn't even know those bad things about him! You reckon she doesn't know? Oh yes, she knows. Well why is her conversation about him different than yours? Because she loves him! And that covers the multitude of sin!

Hey, why don't you go try to talk to God about my meanness and all my bad points! Then ask Him why and how He could save such a rascal as I, HE LOVES ME! The Devil is the Accuser of the Brethren, but God is Love! Accuser means fault-finder. You see, Christ had said to Peter, "Satan hath desired to sift you as wheat . . . ."

Well what happens when you sift wheat? You shake it until all the good grain goes to the bottom and all you can see is the old chaff. He will shake you up!

Now that's what Satan does! He wants to expose every worthless, no good, dirty, rotten thing about you He can! (And He has lots of help through the criticism of church members about one another!)

Don't let Satan use you as a sifter! Have a fervent love for one another.

The very climax and power of love is seen in how much it can suffer. Jesus is the great illustration of love. He is the very essence of the Father's love. The Old Testament talks about His love; the New Testament shows us His love. Jesus came into this world to show us the Father, and what do we see? We see love!

25

Where do we see the love of Jesus manifested? IN HIS SUFFERING!
We see glimpses of His love in various instances in the Scriptures.

1. At the tomb of Lazarus. The love of God said, "Lazarus, come forth!" If He hadn't been specific, the whole cemetery would have come alive!
2. With the (Samaritan) woman at the well. The love of God said, "I'll give you living water!" He saved her, cleaned her up, changed her life, she was made new!
3. We see it illustrated in the story of the Good Samaritan. A man fell among thieves, was beaten, wounded, and left for dead.
    A. The High Priest came by but His religion wouldn't let Him help the man. He would defile Himself!
    B. The Levite came by and He was running late, was behind schedule, He didn't have time. He was supposed to have already had the temple ready and prepared for the work of the priest.
    C. Luke 10:25-37. But the Good Samaritan dressed his wounds, cleaned him up, took him to the inn, paid his fare in full, and said I'll be back later to check on him.

That is the story of complete redemption; though I was a fallen creature, weak and wounded, sick and sore, bruised and mangled by the fall! Christ, my Lord, picked me up, dressed my wounds, paid my redemption in full, and said I'm coming back! Hallelujah!

We see the Love of Our Lord in the Sacrifices He made!

Luke 23:13-25   John 19:1-6   Isaiah 50:6 and 7   Isaiah 53:3-11

Come Ye Sinners, Poor and Needy

Come ye sinners, poor and needy
Weak and wounded, sick and sore
Jesus ready stands to save you
Full of pity, love, and power

Come ye thirsty, come and welcome
God's free bounty glorify
True belief and true repentance
Every grace that brings you nigh
I will arise and go to Jesus
He will embrace me in His arms
In the arms of my dear Savior
Oh, there are ten thousand charms

"The foxes have holes, the birds of the have nests, but the Son of Man hath not where to lay His head."

"He was despised and rejected by men!"

He had no place to be born. He had to be born in a stable. He had no place when He died. He was buried in a borrowed tomb. He walked this earth and had not where to lay His head. "He made Himself of no reputation and became obedient even unto the death of the cross." His obedience was to whom? It was to the Father indicating a divine plan set in motion and operating.

Isaiah 53:3

John 13:31-38

Our Lord left the glory of the Father and came into this world <u>to suffer</u>! He suffered throughout His earthly life, but His suffering became intense as He neared the cross and as He walked out into the Garden of Gethsemane that night.

As He was taken from the Garden of Gethsemane, eventually He wound up facing a mock trial and standing before Pilate. Pilate questioned Him, then said, "I find no fault in Him." But that bloodthirsty mob said, "<u>CRUCIFY HIM</u>!" Pilate's wife had had a terrible dream which she told Pilate about, and Pilate then turned Him over to the Roman Soldiers, and they scourged Him. At that very moment there were more than 12 Legions of Angels (72,000) looking on who Christ could have called!

Edersheim says: This is that same angelic host that had rejoiced the night of His birth. It was an envoy of this heavenly host that had come and strengthened Him when He was tempted in the wilderness. It was an envoy of this heavenly host that had strengthened Him in the Garden of Gethsemane! But here they stood, helpless as they looked on in Pilate's Hall that night! It wasn't that they didn't have the Power. Any single angel could have destroyed the entire Roman Army! For in the Old Testament one single angel had single-handedly destroyed 186,000 soldiers of Sennacharib's Army in one night! But this night they were powerless to do anything. Why? <u>Because Jesus had resigned Himself to become helpless</u>, therefore that paralyzed the angelic host. He came to die! His entire purpose of His life was His death! <u>He resigned Himself to become a lamb and as a lamb He had to be slaughtered</u>! He's the Lord of Heaven and Earth, and <u>the angels couldn't come unless He said come</u>! The angels are paralyzed except at the command of our Lord! So the angels stood by helpless. When God answers your prayer He dispatches angels, commands them to your needs.

If that was the wonder of wonders the night of His birth, the wonder of wonder of all wonders was the night our Savior suffered at the hands of sinners! (Revelation 19:15 ". . . He treadeth the winepress of the wrath of God.") When Pilate turned Him over to the Roman soldiers. THEY WERE MASTERS OF TORTURE!

Calvary was the place where-

The lamb was slaughtered!
The wrath of God punished sin!

1. They plucked the beard from His face!
2. They beat Him until His face was marred, beaten beyond human recognition.
3. They spat upon Him.
4. They smote Him with the reed!
5. They placed a crown of thorns on His head.
6. They scourged Him with a cat 'o nine tails.
7. They placed upon Him a purple robe!

Jesus knew all this was going to befall Him through His divine foreknowledge.

Now we can understand <u>what Jesus saw</u> over there earlier in the Garden and why He was <u>hysterical with screams and shed floods of tears</u>! And why the angel came to strengthen Him! He knew what things He would suffer!

It was customary at Passover time that a prisoner was to be released. Pilate then turned to the multitude standing there and said, "Behold the Man! I'm supposed to release one today. Whom should I release?" And that bloodthirsty mob picked the "Charles Manson" of their day and said, "Release Barabbas, but crucify Him! Pilate took a bowl and washed his hands with water and said, "I find no fault with Him, [I'm not responsible] I'm free from the blood of this Man." And they cried, "Let His Blood Be upon us and our children." In other words, "You Don't Have to be Responsible. We'll take full responsibility. Crucify Him!" And that blood is still required at their hands to this day! This gives us some clearer understanding of why God divorced physical Israel, put her away, and turned to the gentiles and made of them Spiritual Israel; made of them "The Branch Grafted In!"

Pilate, that sinful heathen ruler had more of a knowledge of Jesus and more of a kind and compassionate heart than that throng of religious Pharisees and Scribes and High Priests. And it hasn't changed. It's still that way today! They were the ones who ran the orthodox religion of that day, BUT THEY DIDN'T KNOW WHO CHRIST WAS AND DIDN'T CARE TO KNOW. ALL THEY WANTED WAS FOR HIM TO BE CRUCIFIED. And it's still true today. The Bible said, ". . . they know you not because they knew Him not." They'll hate you because they hated Him! "Oh, preacher, they don't hate me." I DARE YOU TO MAKE AN ABSOLUTE PUBLIC STAND FOR CHRIST! You'll find out! Be different, separated from the world, and cry out against sin and all the worldly competitions to Christianity and the Church. YOU'LL SEE!

That lack of popularity will become HATE! They Hated Christ. Therefore, they Crucified Him! And it was the religious crowd! The sinners accepted Him! You try to live a life separated unto Christ, AND YOU'LL GET MORE SYMPATHY FROM A DRUNKARD!

You preach grace, marvelous grace, saving grace, life-changing grace, grace that teaches you to live soberly, righteously, godly in this present world. The out and out lost sinners will expect you to be different, separated unto Christ, but the religious world hates it! AND THE FIRST ONES TO TURN ON YOU WILL BE THE RELIGIOUS BUNCH! Those who want to play church! The ones who just go to church on Sunday to soothe their conscience! They that think more of their card parties, and fishing boats, and golf clubs than they do the House of God. They think more of their dirty jokes, filthy talk, and foul language than they do their testimony. They think more of their sock hops and juke joints and night clubs and beer and wine and social drinks than they do Jesus! To them salvation is a fire escape. If you don't believe it, tell them all that stuff is sinful and fleshly, and hellish, AND THEY'LL BE READY TO CRUCIFY YOU!

You go through a crisis or two, and it won't take you long to realize you won't get any sympathy from religious folks! THEY'LL CRUCIFY YOU! You may not like what I'm about to say, but you'll get more compassion on a barstool than you will from most church pews! God help us to love people!

After the scourging of our Lord, they made Him bear His cross through the streets and up Golgotha's Hill. With His back and stomach laid open from the scourging, with fresh blood dripping from His lacerated body, and strips of flesh dangling to His knees, they placed that heavy cross right into those open gashes, right upon raw open nerves and muscle, and the exposed bone!

And He bore His cross alone up Calvary's Hill.
He laid Himself upon the cross.
The nails were driven through His hands and feet. He was a dying Lamb. At the Crucifixion He was a swollen, bloody mess.

They dropped the cross into a prepared hole. And when they did, the weight of His body caused Him to lunge forward and all the weight of His body was supported by the wrist and arm muscles! And a spike through the feet. What an agonizing death!

The legs of the crucified ones were broken so they would die quickly! He came for this purpose! They didn't want them on the cross on the "feast" day (Feast of Unleavened Bread). When the soldier came to Jesus to break His legs, He was already dead. Normally it took 3 days, but Christ died in less than 6 hours.

Our Lord had no broken bones. He called Death to do His bidding. (He gave up the Ghost.)

He was taken from the cross and placed in a borrowed tomb. On the 3rd and <u>appointed</u> day, at exactly the right day and exactly the right hour, planned in the council halls of eternity, He rose again!

"The stone rolled away and the Rock of Ages walked out!

And now once a year, Tuesday before Easter, after 6 o'clock PM, the church should get together and observe the Lord's Supper AS A MEMORIAL TO HIM!

Chapter 5

The Darkness of Calvary

Matthew 27:45

Now from the sixth hour there was darkness
over all the land unto the ninth hour.
John 19:19-27

We take so lightly the suffering and death of our Lord on Calvary. In this modern age we evidently do not understand the hopelessness of our fall in Adam. When we realize the hopelessness of the fall, we'll realize the greatness of His suffering and death to redeem us from the fall.

As our Lord was hanging on the cross, not everyone standing around Him was God haters. There were a few who loved Him. Multitudes were there, and multitudes passed by that day who were critics and ridiculers of our Lord. But there was a little handful there who was deeply sorrowed over the suffering and death of Jesus. There are those who think Mary was the center of attention that day; but not so! Despite what the Catholics say, <u>Jesus Christ</u>, the Lord of Glory, had the full attention of <u>all</u> on earth and in heaven. Men viewed Him, the angelic host viewed Him, and <u>God Almighty viewed Him</u>! Not Mary, but <u>HIM</u>! Mary had nothing whatsoever to do with Salvation and Redemption!

If only God in His grace, will allow us to enter into that scene around the cross, and let us view our suffering and dying Lord!

There was some praying going on that day. First, Jesus prayed. "Father, forgive them." And secondly, from all I can learn from the Greek texts this phrase was in a tense which made it repetitious. (The aorist or perfect tense.) In other words, He kept on praying and kept on praying . . . . And the words of the two malefactors on either side of Him are in the same tense; therefore they too <u>kept on</u> praying.

One saying, "If thou be the Son of God, save Thyself and us." And the other one kept on saying, "Lord, remember me when Thou comest into Thy kingdom!"

Let's see if we can, by God's grace, get the proper picture of that scene.

The crowds, the multitudes were standing around or passing by, scoffing, mocking and ridiculing Him. Suddenly through the crowd comes one, pushing and shoving his way through. It is John that disciple whom Jesus loved, and he is leading Mary the Mother of Jesus with him. When the Roman cross was placed in the prepared hole, the feet of the victim were only about 2 feet off the ground. Therefore, one could walk right up to the crucified ones. Among other things, this close up view served as a public example to anyone who would dare defy the laws of Roman Government.

John then, led Mary right up to Jesus that day, so that she could see Him one last time in His agony before He died.

As Mary and John approach the cross, we hear Jesus speak; He made another utterance in the midst of His agony and He addresses first His mother. Some would think surely He was giving her some special place in His kingdom, but not so! Not even a position of a mediator was given her! She was not called the mother of God, nor was she called the Queen of Heaven. When Jesus spoke, He did not call her mother. He called her woman. As He nodded toward John, He said, "Woman, behold thy son." And He said to John, "Son, behold thy mother." There was not one reference to His love for her, not one reference of His devotion to her. Not one reference to any special emotional tie. Jesus was placing His mother here on the level with all other human beings. He called her WOMAN! For Calvary was not the place for fleshly emotional ties, it was the place for the love of God. A place where the Lamb was being slaughtered. We learn here that there is no respecter of persons with God! And when He said, "John, behold thy mother," He was placing her care, her earthly welfare into the hands of John. You see, our Lord was telling Mary where she really stood in the realm of humanity and God. SHE WAS JUST LIKE EVERYBODY ELSE! It takes the same grace of God to save the very mother of Jesus as the thief hanging by His side! When it came to salvation, to redemption, she was no different than anyone else! And in this utterance He was letting her know this in no uncertain terms.

And just shortly after this utterance the Scripture records for us something very unusual that happened. The sun was darkened and a darkness fell over the dreadful site.

Luke 23:44-45

Remember the Jewish day began at 6 PM. God particularly wanted us to know the hour. The sixth hour was twelve noon. And there was darkness over the earth until the ninth hour. (3 o'clock)

There were six miracles that occurred at Calvary that we should take note of
1. The Darkness
2. The Rending of the veil
3. The earthquake and the rocks rending
4. The graves of many were opened
5. The condition inside the tomb of the risen Lord (the napkin was folded)
6. The resurrection of departed saints

Every one of the miracles was connected with the death of our Lord. Some came from Heaven; some came from the earth; some came from under the earth! Remember this when you study the Book of Revelation. All these wonders defend the great truth of our redemption in His blood!

Pray now that God will let you enter into this great scene. They had taken Jesus from the Garden of Gethsemane that night, kept Him up all night, shuffled Him back and forth between Herod and Pilate, scourged Him until He was a bloody pulp, a bloody mass, beaten Him beyond human recognition. Then they hung Him on the cross about 9 o'clock in the morning. The space of about 3 hours had passed and as the noon hour rolled around, suddenly darkness covered the land. Luke said it covered the earth. Matthew said it covered the land. Either way it was a miracle!

This wasn't the first time this had happened! Go back to Exodus chapter 10 to the time God brought darkness to the land of Egypt, a darkness that could be felt. And it lasted for 3 days and 3 nights, while at the same time down in the camp of Goshen where the Israelites were, there was light for the same period of time. What a miraculous display of God, for no matter how bright the sun shone, it would not get light. While in the camp of Goshen, it would not get dark, even if the sun did set, it remained light! What a miraculous display of the sovereignty of God! He is in control!

31

This darkness at Calvary was <u>NOT</u> an eclipse of the sun. The time of the Passover was during the time of the full moon, and it's impossible to have an eclipse during a full moon because the heavenly bodies are not stationed right.

This darkness was not due to the absence of the sun. It was <u>High Noon</u>!

Here was a darkness that was the antagonist of light! Natural light makes darkness flee! Here was a supernatural darkness that made the light flee! It had to be a miraculous act of God! Here was a darkness that smothered out the light of Noonday!

It was not a slow gradual darkness. It was a <u>sudden</u> darkness, by the space of 3 hours. What a miracle!

First 3 hours

Hear our Lord uttering, "Father forgive them." The railing thief, the multitude of scoffers wagging their heads saying, "He can save others but He cannot save Himself!"

The Roman soldiers scoffing Him and dividing His garments and gambling.

Why would they want His garments? Because it was the bloodiest thing they had ever seen. Then there was the argument over the "accusation" Pilate had written. This is Jesus, "King of the Jews." John 19:19-22

<u>Suddenly</u> in the hour when the sun was at its brightest it became <u>terribly dark</u>! A frightful darkness. And the Roman soldiers and the centurions feared greatly. What a terrifying experience. For suddenly there engulfed that scene a deep, terrifying silence. All you could hear was the dripping of the blood of our Lord, and the moans and groans of those crucified ones (perhaps hundreds) around Him on Golgotha.

Tertullian, that Greek historian said, "At the moment of Christ's death the light departed from the Sun, and the land was darkened at noon; and this wonder is related in your own annals, and preserved in your own archives unto this day."

What a miracle of God!

A darkness and a silence fell over the land. Not a ray of light, not a song from a bird, the crickets even hushed! Silence! Hear the groans, hear the blood drops and soak the parched ground! I can see men start to tremble, some begin to cry, and I can hear that Roman officer say "surely this must be the Son of God!"

Can we not understand, God came down and heaven bowed to Him. He came with darkness under His feet and redeemed fallen ruined sinners! In Him we have redemption through His blood! We are not redeemed with corruptible things but with the precious blood of Christ.

<u>God wasn't caught in a bind whereas He didn't have any other choice; neither was Calvary an afterthought of God</u>! Jesus came into this world with one purpose in mind, to redeem Himself a people. And that purpose was set in order before the foundation of the world.

Friends, I have been pardoned!

When President Nixon was about to be impeached, he resigned his position as president of the United States. Vice president Gerald Ford assumed the office. His first official act as president was to give a full pardon to his predecessor. That closed the books! No matter what evidence could have been presented against President Nixon, it was to no avail! He had been pardoned by the highest official in the nation! Glory to God! <u>The Highest Sovereign in the creation has pardoned me</u>!

He pardoned me for the sins of the past, the present, the future! The pardon was secured at Calvary!

What does that have to do with this darkness at Calvary? <u>It was during this darkness that God laid upon Him the chastisement of our peace! He bore the wrath of God, and He became sin for us! And God hid that from public view! He was bruised by God! We could see what</u>

men did to Him, but God would not allow us to see what He did to Him! God punished Sin in Christ! The wrath of God was exhausted that day on Christ! For He became SIN!

And this was worked out between the Father and the Son before the foundation of the world! Christ didn't suffer the reproach of men and the wrath of God perchance that someday, someone might possibly accept Him! NO! He was redeeming Himself a people! Elect according to the foreknowledge of God!

God purposed to redeem Himself a people out of Adam's fallen race and conform them to the image of His Son! AND THAT REDEMPTION WAS MADE SECURE, MADE SURE AT CALVARY! This was the New Covenant of Salvation by grace through His blood! This wasn't a covenant made with Abraham; this was the fulfilling of that covenant made between the Father and the Son, before the foundation of the world!

The sealing of this covenant was made with the blood of the Son of God, as He who knew no sin became sin, and suffered the eternal wrath of God for his elect people, His church, His bride!

Christ satisfied the travail of the Soul of God!

Once sin entered into the human race, God had to do something with Adam and Adam's race. God's justice cries for damnation, His mercy cries for salvation! Once sin entered, the choice was no longer Adam's but God's! And God is still doing something with Adam! Every man, woman, boy, and girl is viewed by God either in Adam or in Christ! In Adam, you'll go to hell and suffer the wrath of God eternally for your sin! In Christ, He paid the sin debt for you and will take you to His heaven! So I ask you the question: WHERE ART THOU?

IN ADAM OR IN CHRIST? Christ died as a good Shepherd. Not for wolves, not for goats, but for His sheep!

Chapter 6

The New Covenant of Atonement!

Romans 5:11
Matthew 26:26-28

The Lord's Supper is not a communion nor is it a sacrament. When the Lord spoke of a New Covenant, He was referring to a covenant of grace made sure by Atonement. He was that night looking back upon the work of that Old Testament High Priest knowing that He was <u>our</u> High Priest! There are 2 essential points that are imperative for us to know;

1. We do not wait until the Lord's Supper to commune with Him.
2. Nothing divine is imparted to us through it; neither does the wine and bread turn into the literal body and blood of our Lord. (Transubstantiation)

ON CALVARY, CHRIST FULFILLED THE LAW! WHAT DOES THAT MEAN? HOW? HE BECAME THE HIGH PRIEST, THE OLD TESTAMENT HIGH PRIEST WAS ONLY A TYPE OF OUR LORD JESUS CHRIST, WHO CAME AND LITERALLY FULFILLED THE LAW OF ATONEMENT!

On the Day of Atonement the high priest went alone into the tabernacle and went into the Holy of Holies. (Leviticus 16:17 Only one man could go!) He was going to do something that only one man could do. First He ceremoniously cleansed Himself, (Christ is clean and perfect!) then He made a sin offering for the people, prayed the sins of Israel on a goat, then had it carried away into the wilderness, far enough away so that it would never again return into the camp of Israel. This was the scapegoat. There were other ceremonies the high priest went through, all under the Old Covenant. But Christ fulfilled the Old Covenant and men would no longer have to go through such ceremonies, for He made a New Covenant upon His death at Calvary, He as the great high priest performed a work of redemption once and for all. To make sure that NO priest would go behind that veil again, it was rent (torn) apart at the crucifixion of our Lord.

When the high priest went into the Holy of Holies to make a sacrifice for Israel, the duration of that law was one year. (Exodus 39) When the priest clothed himself on his garment was sewn a bell and a pomegranate all around the border. Also a rope was tied around his ankle stretched under the tent out into the congregation. Whatever happened to him happened to them. They were <u>at-one</u> with him.

On that great Day of Atonement, talking about that Day when all of Israel became <u>at-one</u> with the priest. He was going into the Holy of Holies, but they were <u>at-one</u> with him. He was going to offer a sacrificial lamb and they were <u>at-one</u> with him. If the lamb was accepted or not accepted, they were <u>at-one</u> with him. However God regarded that high priest is how they were regarded! They were <u>at-one</u> with him! The word Atonement means "AT-ONE-MENT."

They were identified with all that high priest did. The congregation was regarded through the work of that priest. When the ceremony was complete the whole congregation remained silent, was the sacrifice accepted? Were their sins forgiven? They were at-one with the priest! When the sacrifice was accepted, the Shekinah glory of God would fall, and the bells sewn into the hem of his garment began to ring! They were accepted, forgiven. The sin offering was accepted! How did they know? Ask them and they would answer, "We have heard the joyful sound!"

Had they been to the inner court? No, but the priest had. And they were at-one with him. Had they been behind the veil? No, but he had and they were at-one with him. Had they seen the fire of God fall in the Holy of Holies accepting and consuming the sacrifice? No, but he had, and they were at-one with him! This is the basis of the whole redemption story: Atonement! For that Old Testament priest represents Christ! As the High Priest represented the people, Christ represents Me! My redemption, my assurance rests in Him, in the priest!

Have I been in the Garden of Gethsemane praying until my sweat became as great drops of blood? NO, BUT HE HAS! Have I stood in Pilate's Hall in a mock trial? NO, BUT HE HAS! And I am At One With Him. Have I stood before a railing multitude and heard them say Crucify Him? NO, BUT HE HAS! And I am at-one with Him!

Have I been nailed to a rugged wooden cross and suspended between heaven and earth? NO, BUT HE HAS! And I am at-one with Him! Have I suffered the wrath of God, poured out upon me and has God exhausted His wrath upon me for what I am? NO, BUT HE HAS! Christ became Sin, and suffered the fury, the wrath of a holy God until that wrath was exhausted. And I am at-one with Him!

Have I ever died, literally, totally, and been placed in a tomb and sealed in at the command of the King? NO, BUT HE HAS! And I am at-one with Him! Have I ever risen from the grave and ascended to the Father? NO, BUT HE HAS! And I am at-one with Him! Can I stand before God and hope to be accepted in His eternal holy presence? NO, BUT HE HAS and IS! And I am at-one with Him! Hallelujah!

Atonement has been made! I am accepted in Christ! Not in my own merit but in Him! Not in my goodness, my works, my righteousness, BUT I AM AT-ONE with Him! This will do you in your dying hour! At-one with Him! If I had but one message to preach to this sin-cursed world, this is it- Atonement! My redemption does not depend on me nor on my works at all, but upon Him and His work! And His Work is Acceptable, Accomplished, Completed! It is Finished! Never again will a lamb have to be slain! Christ was the lamb slain once and for all! We now have a New Covenant of Grace! Our Salvation no longer depends on works. But it depends on His grace! I am not saved, nor kept saved by my works – But it's grace! The Doctrine of Atonement tells us we are represented in our federal head! God views you either in Adam or in Christ! If you are found in Adam, you will suffer all the sins of Adam's race! And Hell will be your eternal destiny!

I used to be viewed in Adam! Identified with Adam, for I was born into the race of Adam. Born in sin, shapen in iniquity, came into this world speaking lies. I was a member of Adam's race. I inherited everything Adam brought with him out of the garden, which was the curse of sin and death! I was a sinner by faith, a sinner by choice, a sinner at will, a sinner by nature, a sinner by imputation! God charged me with the sins of all of Adam's race! When you ever find out there's no inequality in the family of God, you'll find out there's no inequality in Adam's race either! Whatever Hitler did, you're going to pay for! Where does that put the doctrine of degrees of heat in Hell and degrees of reward in heaven if you're at one with your federal head?

In my natural birth! I am viewed in Adam! Just as it doth not yet appear what we shall be as children of God, it doth not appear what Adam's race will be! But they'll know one day for they'll wind up in Hell, Guilty, Guilty, Guilty in Adam! God didn't just look at the sin I committed, He looked at the sin I was capable of committing. Do you know the reason that two boys can't lift as much as two men? It's because they're not grown yet. You let them grow up and they'll lift just as much! You frown at the prostitute, the dope pusher, the drug addict, but put you under the right circumstances and you'll commit worse sins than they do! And be meaner than they are. I was doomed, because father Adam was doomed and I'm doomed, fallen, guilty in him! I am under the same guilt, the same condemnation as Adam! Headed for Hell, fallen, a rebel, against God!

How will I make it to Heaven?

How am I to be saved?

Christ is my surety! I couldn't pay, so He paid!

I have been saved by grace through faith. Now I am in Christ! God no longer views me in Adam, He views me in Christ! I am now identified with the Risen Savior! He is my High Priest, and however God regards Him, He regards me! If He's pure, I'm pure; if He's righteous, I'm righteous; if He's holy, I'm holy!

If you don't believe in holiness, you'd better get hold of this, for the Bible says without holiness, no man shall see God! Now if you don't have any holiness, you'd better find out where you can get some! Without it you'll not see God! Praise God! Christ has all the holiness I need and I'm in Him. Hallelujah!

I am no longer guilty! I am no longer condemned! My surety has paid my debt! The debt is paid in full, satisfied! And right now, I am just as holy as Christ is holy! I'm just as righteous in the eyes of God. I AM AT-ONE WITH HIM! He has satisfied the wrath of God and since we are in AT-ONE-MENT, God will never demand anything more from me. The wrath of God is satisfied! In ME? NO! IN HIS SON!

God is not mad at me anymore! I'm as pure as if I'd never sinned! And not of works, it's a gift! It's by grace! Through faith! AND THAT NOT OF YOURSELVES, IT IS THE GIFT OF GOD!

Christ didn't come into the world to condemn the world, because the world was condemned already!

Something had to be done to take us out from under that condemnation!

(John 3:18) "But he that believeth on Him (the Son of God), Shall Not Be Condemned!"

(John 6:37) "All that the Father giveth Me shall come to Me. And him that cometh to Me, I will not cast out!"

Our Salvation is a Covenant between the Father and the Son.

There is an elect bride given to Christ as a love gift from the Father! And she shall not be cast out! She shall be brought in without spot or blemish!

Hey, I am identified with Him! In the eyes of God, I have been in Him from the foundation of the world!

Does that mean I'm sinless? Oh No, I battle this flesh every day. I am constantly repenting and pleading with God over my sin! This old Adam nature is still here. But Christ made a New Covenant; He cast my sins behind His back. He put them away as far as the east is from the west! He paid for All my sins!

"If we confess our sins, He is faithful and just to forgive us our sins and cleanse us from all unrighteousness!" 1 John 1:9

We Are Justified!

Though we are sinners, when we come to Christ, God views me as "Just if I'd never sinned!" (JUSTIFIED) In what is my hope? My hope is in His blood! He is my high priest. And we are AT-ONE-MENT!

Saved by <u>Grace</u>.

Not of works at all.

Your <u>works</u> do not impress God!

Christ's <u>work</u> impresses God!

Sin is not something you do. Sin is a principle. It is what you are! And the only way we can ever escape condemnation is through Him! IN HIM! BY HIM! The only way we can be <u>liberated</u> is by the Grace of God!

If all you get is a good case of religion, in just a little while you'll be over there a big wheel in the church, making rules and regulations for everybody to live by according to your standard! <u>But if you ever find Christ, you'll realize you don't have anything to lift up a standard with</u>! You'll see yourself as nobody and nothing, and Christ as everything!

Come clean with God! Quit trying to impress <u>God</u>, and just come as you are. Quit trying to impress <u>people</u>! Come clean with God!

Agree with God about your sin.

Confess it to Him!

And the blood of Jesus Christ His Son will cleanse you and wash you whiter than snow!

Then you can be <u>At-One-Ment</u> with God! And your sins will be Atoned.

Chapter 7

The Cup of Blessing

Matthew 26:26-30

26 And as they were eating, Jesus took bread, and blessed it, and brake it, and gave it to the disciples, and said, Take, eat; this is my body.
27 And he took the cup, and gave thanks, and gave it to them, saying, Drink ye all of it;
28 For this is my blood of the new testament, which is shed for many for the remission of sins.
29 But I say unto you, I will not drink henceforth of this fruit of the vine, until that day when I drink it new with you in my Father's kingdom.
30 And when they had sung an hymn, they went out into the mount of Olives.

Luke 22:13–20
1 Corinthians 5:6–8
1 Corinthians 10:16

Two things have always separated Baptists from all other denominations. They are (1.) their staunch doctrine concerning the ordinances of Baptism and (2.) the ordinance of the Lord's Supper. When the Bible said to "show forth His death till He come," it means "showing ahead of time." How far ahead? Go back into the Old Testament, back to the Garden, and see Christ, the lamb slain from the foundation of the world. Christ has shown forth His death since the Garden of Eden.

We are chosen, in Him, and for Him. We are at-one with Him. He is our high priest. Christ, our Passover, was sacrificed for us – once and for all.

As a result of Old Testament Israel trusting the blood of a lamb, there was great deliverance. All who trusted the slain lamb were set free! Have you trusted the Lamb? Are you free from the bondage of sin and death? He is our Passover!

(Ephesians 1:13) "In whom also ye also trusted after ye heard the word of truth, ye were sealed with that Holy Spirit of promise." The Holy Spirit always operates according to, or with, a promise! Their promise in Egypt was one of deliverance! And the promise went on to say, "ye shall be my people and I will be your God."

And God said you are to set this up as a memorial to me – every year! Now later as Israel grew, and became a nation; and established a capitol. And the temple was built; they were then instructed that every family would send a male representative from their household to Jerusalem. At Passover time either the head of the household, the father, or the firstborn son was required to go to Jerusalem to represent his family. What was Christ doing in Jerusalem that year? He was the "firstborn of many brethren!" He is the Heavenly Father of an elect church. He is God the Father and God the Son!

The Passover was observed each year, with the slaying of a lamb.
Every year it memorialized some things for them.
1. It memorialized their great and glorious deliverance from the bondage they were under.
2. The bitter herbs that they ate memorialized their affliction.
3. It memorialized that they were set free by the blood of a lamb. The blood alone was their only hope.
4. It memorialized that they were a people with freedom and hope, because they had been claimed by God. As His own peculiar treasure! And it was <u>all settled in the blood of the lamb</u>. They were "<u>elected</u>" by Him!

They slew the lamb as a divinely ordered sacrifice. Every year the head of the household would slay a lamb, take it to a Levite priest, who would take the blood of it and sprinkle it on the altar. The household representative, would then take the lamb home, roast it with fire, and eat it with His family. <u>And this was done every year</u>.

Note: The head of the household or the firstborn son was responsible for his family!

Later in the New Testament it was brought to the apostles' attention that widows and orphans needed a representative and deacons were appointed. They stood in the place of the household head for those who didn't have one.

But we don't kill animals anymore. We don't have to for Christ was once (once and for all) offered. And "there remaineth <u>no more sacrifice</u> for sin." There's no need of it! Christ our lamb was sacrificed for us. He is the Passover!

The Passover brought all of Israel together on <u>common</u> <u>ground</u> every year. One may have been wealthy, another poor, but every year they were to come together on one common ground. And remembered <u>together</u> that the blood of the Lamb was their only hope! And that's what the celebration of the Passover is all about, remembering together that the blood of the Lamb is our only hope!

The Passover was a weeklong assembly. The Lord called it in the Old Testament a "Holy Convocation" which means a "Solemn Sacred Assembly." <u>Remember</u> this was a very solemn, sacred assembly. They had a seven day convocation. Seven signifies <u>completion</u>! The sacrifice of the Lamb <u>completely</u> delivered them! And we are <u>completely</u> delivered, and His work is <u>completely</u> finished. We are <u>completely</u> saved by the Blood of the Lamb – Our Passover. (Who is Christ!) What a blessing it is when we follow this same order! For seven days they were to have nothing else on their mind except their deliverance, that night of the Passover.

They memorialized God's mercy on them by delivering them from such great bondage! Therefore, the memorial of the Lord's Supper is also a memorial of God's <u>mercy on sinners</u>, <u>great sinners</u>, <u>such as we are</u>!

In John chapter 4, our Lord said to a crowd of people, "except ye eat the flesh of the Son of God, and drink His blood ye have no life!" We must then recognize our eternal nourishment and strength comes from Christ our Passover! He is our life! The sacrificial Lamb had to be pure and spotless; it had to be without a blemish. This was a picture of our Lord who was holy and undefiled.

When He was tried by the law, the law could find no fault with Him. When He was tried by the world, they said, "We find nothing worthy of death in this man." When He was dying between the two malefactors, they said "We are dying justly for our sins, but this Man hath done nothing amiss." And the Roman soldiers that drove the spikes through His hands, feared and trembled, and said, "Surely this Man was the Son of God."

The doctrine of God's sovereign grace is such a precious glorious doctrine! The doctrine of God's sovereign grace simply says, "Salvation is not in us, it's in Him!" And that doesn't encourage people to live loosely! Oh, can you not see that precious truth of the Scripture which tells us we are chosen in Him before the foundation of the world! How can that be? Because He was the Lamb slain from the foundation of the world, and He was slain to redeem Himself a people! That night of the Passover, Israel was an elect people from the midst of Egypt. God had a people in mind and in plan. The foundation of our redemption rests in this! Our hope rests in this! When our Lord went to Calvary, as our Passover Lamb, He had a people in mind and in plan! He was redeeming Himself a church! A particular people, elect unto Him! If you are ever touched by His grace, and really get a revelation of who Christ was, and what He came to do, and that His work is accomplished, it will humble you before Him! You'll not stand and argue the doctrine of election and predestination; you'll be too humbled over the fact that God brought you in! If God's grace ever bursts faith into your soul, and His Son revealed in your heart, you'll want to be more like Christ. You'll have a desire to live and act holy unto Him! Repentance is not a onetime thing for the child of God; He constantly repents, for He is at war with this old nature! The children of God cannot glory in their shame, their sin! Oh NO! Grace teaches us to deny ungodliness, and worldly lusts, and live soberly righteously, and godly in this present world!

You see, the Doctrine of Sovereign Grace Teaches Us that We have offended God! You have . . . . I have . . . . We are fallen and we are sinners, and God is offended! In the Old Testament, this is why the sacrificial law was set in order. AND IT WAS GOD HIMSELF WHO SET IT IN ORDER IN THE GARDEN OF EDEN! Sacrifices were appointed of God ever since the fall. We are fallen creatures and God appointed a sacrifice for us. The only way we can hope to approach God is through the proper blood sacrifice. WE'VE GOT TO HAVE A LAMB TO OFFER!

Christ is our sacrifice. HE IS OUR LAMB – SALVATION FROM SIN IS MERELY OFFERING GOD THE PROPER ACCEPTABLE SACRIFICE! We must understand, when the Old Testament Animal of Sacrifice was brought, it was slain, it died, it was representing the one who had offended God! The wages of sin is death! It demands death! Either I die, or my sacrifice dies. Christ is our sacrifice – our Passover! That sacrificial animal died in the stead of that one who had offended God! The bringing of a sacrifice was a testimony that he who was offering it was a sinner, and had forfeited His right to God. That's what sin did, it caused you to forfeit your right to God! Adam is the federal head, and we've fallen in him. He's the Poison Spring head. If Adam hadn't have fallen, you would. You've proved it over and over!

Christ died the just for the unjust; a dying animal could not take our sins away, but Christ died and He took our sins away and cast them . . .

1. behind His back; and in him is no variableness, nor shadow of turning,
2. in the sea of forgetfulness, never to be remembered,
3. as far as the east is from the west.

And there need be no more sacrifice. There remaineth no more sacrifice. He was sacrificed for us and He is called our Passover!

This dear friends, gives God's people the deepest ground of humiliation, for we recognize that our right to God is forfeited. We can never go to where God is, He must come to us. And if He never comes to you, you'll burn eternally in Hell! Friends, Christ's death on Calvary wrought for us a great deliverance, and that is the grounds for a most sublime joy. THAT'S WHY WE CELEBRATE. WE'VE BEEN DELIVERED FROM THE BONDAGE OF SIN AND DEATH!

So Paul said, "Let us, therefore keep the feast!" Let's keep it! And observe it properly, and seriously and solemnly, and sacredly and joyfully! Our Lord said keep it. Moses told Israel to keep it. There's a remnant of Jews left trying to keep it. The Jews can't Biblically keep it anymore, for Israel fell! But the church can keep it! Ten tribes were carried off into Assyria as captives and destroyed. Nobody ever heard of them again. Only the tribes of Judah and Benjamin and a handful of Levites remained. Our Lord came through the tribe of Judah or it would have been destroyed too! If only you could understand that we, the church are now spiritual Israel. We make up the Kingdom of God. How? 1. We have a King who rules us sovereignly, and supremely – that is Christ. 2. We have a high priest – who is Christ. 3. We have a sacrifice – who is Christ our Lamb! 4. We have a capital city which is New Jerusalem, and is a Holy City for Spiritual Israel to inhabit! Old Testament Israel is type and shadow of Christ – and His Church!

But Christ came on the scene literally to fulfill all prophecy, all Scripture, all types and shadows concerning Him. He kept all the laws and commandments of Israel, and kept all the appointments (feasts) and traditions of the Jews. He came to Jerusalem. This last week He was on earth, to observe the Passover! At that time of year Jerusalem was packed – probably around 3 million people in Jerusalem to observe this week of Holy Convocation, (up to 6 times its normal population.)

Jesus said to His disciples, go to a certain house and tell a certain man that we will partake of the Supper there.

(Remember this began way back in Egypt. God delivered them mightily through the blood of the Lamb.) (See Exodus 12)

The disciples had met the servant with the pitcher of water. They had delivered their message to the master of the house and they had seen the large upper room furnished and ready. And now it was approaching time for the evening service and sacrifice.

The priests' court was filled with white robed priests and Levites. Before the incense was burnt for the evening sacrifice the paschal lambs were slain. A threefold blast from the priests' trumpet intimated that the lambs were being slain. Each head of household did this for himself and his family. The priests stood in two rows at the great Altar of burnt offering. As one caught up the blood of the dying lamb in a golden bowl, he handed it to his colleague, receiving in return an empty bowl. And so the blood was passed on to the great Altar where it was sprinkled (Greek: proschusis: poured) at the base of the Altar. While this was going on the Levites were chanting the "Hallel." The first line of each "Hallel" was repeated by the worshipers, and to every other line they responded with "Hallelujah." It was probably as the sun was beginning to decline in the horizon that Jesus and the disciples ascended once more the Mount of Olives into the city. Before them lay Jerusalem is her festive attire. White tents could be seen everywhere along with the bright flowers of early spring. From the gorgeous temple buildings dazzling in their snow white marble and gold, arose the smoke of the Altar of burnt offerings. The courts were crowded with eager worshipers offering for the last time in the real sense their paschal lambs. It was the last unhindered and free view our Lord would have of the Holy City until after his resurrection. He was going forward into the city to accomplish His death. To fulfill type and prophecy, and to offer Himself as the true Passover Lamb, the Lamb of God, which taketh away the sin of the world.

And now they were in the city, and ascending the stairs to the upper chamber. The early meal of the Passover week was about to begin.

On that Tuesday evening they entered the upper room, and sat down to begin the Passover meal. Now let me mention here that the meal was eaten in various sessions, or parts. All of it however had to be eaten by Sundown the next night.

Let's look at the Custom and Tradition of the Passover feast.

Customarily they were committed to eat the early meal. They would start out with their bitter herbs, and their wine, and their unleavened bread as the early part of the meal. Their instruction was that they could not meet in companies of less than 10 and no more than 20. Our Lord had 13 in His company and so they began. Judas left before they finished, before they got started good AND THAT LEFT 12 TO PARTAKE OF THE MEAL.

Tuesday evening after 6 o'clock they began this early meal or preparation meal. But the lamb was not to be killed until the next day, then roasted with fire. And they would eat the lamb between 3 o'clock and 6 o'clock when the Passover day ended. This was known as the meal of the lamb. Once the early meal, the preparation meal was completed, the group could disperse, BUT the same group had to meet together again at 3 o'clock the next evening to finish the meal together. The law stated that whoever began the meal together had to reassemble and finish the meal together. You could not start the meal with one group and finish with another. No! You were all partakers together! You had to finish it with the same group you started with! If one were missing, for whatever reason, the entire group had to disperse without finishing the meal and wait until the next year and start again.

Isn't it amazing that our Lord didn't have anybody with Him but the Twelve and by the next morning He was on the cross. Therefore the meal was left unfinished! (More about this later.)

Upon assembling together had the unleavened bread and the sop (made from bitter herbs mixed with wine). They started out the meal though with a cup of wine. Traditionally they had 4 cups of wine altogether in the celebration of the Passover feast. Gamaliel is reported to have said that, "A Jew ought to have 4 cups of wine at the Passover, even if he had to sell his goods." Now, they did not go about this haphazardly, it was in divine order. And we ought to be as strict about The Lord's Supper as They Were about Their Passover Feast! A Lot of things they did, that we don't have to do, because we are now under a New Covenant, and our Lord didn't tell us to keep it the Old Way. Our Lord told us how to keep it, but it will bless us when we understand some things about the old tradition.

The head of the company recited the "Kiddush" or prayer of consecration and thanksgiving for the season. And they drank the first cup. The presiding officer would give a synopsis of Israel's history and God's deliverance from Egypt. Then they sang the first part of the Hallel (Psalm 113 and Psalm 114) and drank the second cup.

(Note: They started out with the first cup of wine. The presiding officer was called the host. He was to continue being president over their assembly until it was all finished the next evening at 6 o'clock. He was responsible to take care of the whole operation of the Passover with his group or company. And our Lord was president or host of His group.)

The presiding officer of the group would greet them, and make a comment. Our Lord's greeting and comment was "For a long time I've wanted to eat this supper with you before I suffer." And He said "Divide this among yourselves and He passed the wine they ceremoniously washed their hands, had the second cup of wine and then ate the sop. They dipped some of the unleavened bread into the sop, and ate some of it. Then they washed again. During this time, Jesus washed their feet to show them He was still in the form of a servant. He said some things about Judas, and Judas then left the group.

With the ceremonial washing of hands, the presiding officer then broke the unleavened bread and pronounced a blessing.

He would pray a prayer of thanksgiving to him who brings forth bread. And pray a prayer of thanksgiving for the commandment to eat unleavened bread. Then the third cup of wine was drunk. This was known as the Cup of Blessing.

After the third cup they recited the second part of the Hallel (Psalm 115-Psalm 118) and dismissed and came back the next day and ate the Roast Lamb. Don't forget this was called the "Meal of the Lamb." After this meal they drank the fourth cup of wine known as the Cup of Praise, and the Cup of Benediction.

Jesus took the bread and said, "Take, eat. This is My body which is broken for you!"

Then they took the third cup of wine, which is referred to as the "Cup of Blessing." Paul even said, "This cup of blessing which we bless." Jesus said, "This is my blood that was shed for many, drink ye all of it."

Now the fourth cup of wine was reserved as the 'Benediction Cup,' and could not be drank until all the Passover was finished and they'd all go back to the house to await again the next year and the next Passover.

They could not drink the fourth cup until everything was finished and they were eating the Roasted Lamb and were looking with anticipation to another year and another Passover. Our Lord took that third cup, the cup of blessing, and said, "This is the blood of the New Covenant." "As oft as ye do this, do it as a memorial unto me." They sang a hymn and went out. The disciples' idea was that they would gather back together the next day, kill and roast their lamb, and they'd eat it together and finish it off with their benediction cup of wine.

You see, it puzzled those disciples when in drinking that cup of blessing, that third cup, Christ said, "I'll drink no more of this fruit of the vine until I drink it anew with you in My Father's Kingdom."

When our Lord was in Gethsemane praying, "Let this cup pass from Me." He was referring to the 4th cup. He was praying that this would be the Passover He was to die on! In hysterical agony and floods of tears He flung Himself on the ground and cried, "Oh, My Father . . . ." And He was heard! This is what He came for!

After the third cup of wine the company dismissed and came back together the next day between 3 and 6 to eat the Roasted Lamb and drank the fourth cup – the benediction cup. Jesus had already drunk the third cup of wine when He went into the Garden of Gethsemane. There was still one more cup to go when He knelt there to pray. AND THAT'S THE CUP HE WAS PRAYING ABOUT!

When we go back to the Garden of Gethsemane and see Christ praying there we find Him nearing the hour of His crucifixion. The grief of that hour drew near when He would be made sin for us, when the Lord would lay upon Him the iniquity of us all. The Scripture said, "He did fear and quake and was grief stricken and exceedingly sorrowful and heavy of heart." He flung Himself on the ground and in great agony, He cried out in hysterical screams and floods of tears, and broken in anguish, prayed, "Oh, My Father, let this cup pass from me! And the Scripture says HE WAS HEARD! And God sent the Angel to strengthen Him! From that point on He was at peace!

But what was He praying for

He was praying His way to Calvary!

He had kept the law, fulfilled all Scripture and all prophecy concerning His coming as Messiah, He had overcome temptation and was now ready to be offered. He prayed, "Father, if it be possible, let this cup pass from Me." He didn't want to wait for another year. He was ready NOW to Go To Calvary. He wanted this to be it! He wanted that fourth Cup of Benediction to pass from Him! That's the cup He was talking about.

The law required that each member of the company had to come together again to finish the meal the next day between 3 and 6 o'clock. If only one were missing – none could partake and the meal was left unfinished. In despair they had to return home immediately – mourning because the meal was unfinished. Not able to join in any more of the festivities until the next year and they would have to start all over!

Where was our Lord by 3 o'clock the next day? Hanging on the cross as a slaughtered Lamb! He left them with one more cup to go, but He told them when He would drink that cup with them again. He said, "I'll drink it anew with you in My Father's Kingdom."

And He was heard! HALLELUJAH!

Psalm 75:8

If you look up the word "cup" in your references in your Bible, you'll find out even the Psalms talk about our Lord coming with a cup! When He returns again, He'll return with a cup! Not for a Benediction – But for the Marriage Supper of the Lamb! We'll partake of the Meal of the Lamb! He'll drink it NEW with us in the Father's Kingdom. We'll sit down together at the Meal of the Lamb! He's coming again and He's coming with a cup!

Well, Glory to God! On the Tuesday night before Easter, after 6 o'clock, the church should call a Holy Convocation to have the Lord's Supper; to memorialize Him and our redemption. Well how oft should we do this? Every year till He comes! For you see the Lord's Supper will not end with the grave! We're still anticipating that fourth cup! That's why we still call it the "Cup of Blessing," because we know we still have one more to go!

He is the Presiding Officer. The Host you see. Those disciples couldn't even reassemble that next day, because their Host was gone. Therefore they had to leave without killing a lamb, without sprinkling blood, without eating the meat, without drinking the fourth cup! The meal was left incomplete, the table left as it was. There's another cup to go, we haven't finished yet!

But Glory to God, the Lamb was slain, the blood was shed, the final meal is being prepared; The Meal of the Lamb – the Marriage Supper of the Lamb. And, Hallelujah, when He returns, He'll return with that cup! It will all be over. The Cup of Benediction will become the Cup of Redemption; the Cup of New Beginnings because it will just be beginning! We will drink the New Cup of the Marriage Supper! He's coming, He's coming and He'll come with a Cup, and we'll drink it new with Him in the Father's Kingdom!

So let us keep the feast! 1 Corinthians 11:24-25.

I'm reminded of the words of the old song, "Come Ye Sinners." Especially the line that says, "Then He'll call us home to heaven at His table we'll sit down (and with the fourth cup in His hand), Christ will gird Himself and serve us with sweet manna all around!

Chapter 8

The Triumph of Calvary or The Necessity of Christ's Death

Matthew 1:21
1 Peter 1:18-20
Romans 5:6-10
Galatians 1:3-5
Colossians 2:15

Nearly two thousand years ago there was an event which took place that was the most momentous occurrence in the history of man. This event divided history, separated time, changed the course of nations, and gave hope to men who otherwise had no hope. This event was the coming of Christ to this earth and ultimately to Calvary. What really happened at Calvary? And how should we look at it through the eyes of those who were present at the crucifixion? Should we look at it through the eyes of today's religious world? OR – SHOULD WE LOOK AT CALVARY AS GOD VIEWS IT? Surely we should view Calvary as much as is possible through the eyes of God in order to understand what really happened there!

When our Lord died, it appeared to the world like a failure and a defeat. Satan thought He had surely triumphed at last and the enemies of our Lord thought for sure that it was the last of Him.

But, my friends, Calvary was <u>not</u> the place of defeat and failure; it was the place of VICTORY, SUCCESS, AND TRIUMPH!

Our text teaches us that Calvary was the field of battle where our Lord fought and won. It is the place where Christ became the mighty Conqueror. <u>There</u>, Christ died for ruined sinners. And everyone for whom Christ died will be redeemed.

Some Unbiblical Concepts of the Purpose of Calvary (<u>False Theories</u>)

First, we must understand that . . .

"The world by Wisdom knows not God."

The cross is foolishness to the religionists who have never been conquered by its power. "The preaching of the cross is foolishness to them that perish."

The Example Concept is not taught in the Bible.

This is the idea that the life and death of Christ was only to serve as an example to inspire us to live and lead a similar life.

Even some of the Eastern religions that deny Christ will go along with this. (He was a good prophet and everyone should learn by His example; then the world would be a better place.) <u>You do not have to accept the Lordship of Christ to believe this!</u>

The Martyr Concept is not taught in the Bible.

This is the idea that Jesus died only to show men that truth is worth dying for, and in so doing became the world's greatest Martyr.

This idea denies that the death of our Lord paid the penalty for sin and advocates that His death was no more effectual in Salvation than any other person who gave their life for a good cause.

This theory engulfs the idea too, that Jesus was an "activist" of His day, and became a Martyr for it.

The "Ransom to Satan" Concept is not taught in the Bible.

This theory teaches that Satan had great and powerful claims on man. And that the death of Christ on the cross was in order to pay the ransom price to Satan. Only by the payment of the just claims of Satan could man be the free possession of God!

This makes Satan to be the great power, the sovereign, and has Christ bowing to the will and wishes of him; paying a ransom to him for the release of the captives!

(Not so! God alone is Sovereign! Friends, Calvary was the place where God crushed sin, punished it, exhausted His wrath, AND SATAN WAS OVERCOME! NOT PAID A RANSOM!)

The General Atonement Concept is not taught in the Bible.

This theory states that Christ provided an atonement for man, then leaves it up to him, and his own fallen nature, and will, as to whether or not he will take advantage of it and accept it.

According to this most popular theory, the death of our Lord did not actually secure the Salvation of anyone, but only made it possible. Please allow me to ask some soul searching questions concerning the general atonement theory . . .

1. Is Salvation a gift or an offer?
2. Did Christ die to make Salvation possible, or to make Salvation sure?
3. Is Salvation totally and completely in the hands of God, or is there a part of it in the hands of man?
4. Do you need to accept Christ, or does God need to accept you?
5. Have you rejected Christ, or has God rejected you?
6. IS HELL A MONUMENT TO THE FAILURE OF GOD?
7. Does the Power of Salvation lie in the hands of God, or in the hands of sinners?
8. Is God doing His best to save everybody? If so, He is obviously defeated, discouraged, and disturbed since multitudes are going to hell anyway.

I want to go on record that I reject such a God dishonoring view!
Galatians 6:14.

General Atonement Is No Atonement at all! And true Christians rejected it until the last century!

Spurgeon said, "General atonement is like a bridge with only half an arch: It doesn't go all the way across the stream. . . ."

To lay Salvation in the hands of sinners, is to open the door for unscriptural schemes to wrest professions of faith from men by human means, thus filling our churches with unregenerate throngs of people!

This creates a religious atmosphere among lost men, fills our churches with goats instead of sheep, and creates a problem for preaching. It fosters apostasy, gives birth to modernism and encourages division.

It leaves no room for the total fall of man and his complete alienation from God.

None of these false theories that I have mentioned glorifies the atoning work of our Savior. They miserably fail in glorifying Him whose blood satisfied the divine justice of God, and whose work alone saves men without anything being added on their part! Salvation is by grace alone!

Whether you are saved or not depends upon whether Christ is your full atonement!

Is He? Is He completely your Passover? Is He your Lamb! Is He your Sacrifice?

The Necessity of Calvary
The Death of Christ was an Absolute Necessity.

God's holiness demands that His Holy Law be satisfied; God's Divine Nature demands that His justice be satisfied. God's Divine Holiness demands that sin cannot stand in His presence. The holiness of the divine character of God demands absolute perfection! Can you produce that? If not, you need a sacrifice. The Only One who could satisfy the demands of God is Christ! His death on Calvary was absolutely necessary because it was part of the sovereign will and purpose of Almighty God!

Calvary was not an afterthought of God, neither was it an emergency provision!

The death of Christ has been part of God's will and purpose from eternity. "Who verily was foreordained before the foundation of the world." 1 Peter 1:18-20 Everything that Christ did at Calvary was foreordained by God!

NONE OF IT WAS BY CHANCE!

God was not obligated to send the world a Savior! He is not obligated to you any more than He is obligated to the angels that sinned, and He didn't provide them a way of escape! II Peter 2:4 says that "God spared not the angels that sinned . . . ."

The Death of Christ at Calvary is the very core of the determination of God! God determined that . . .

> Christ shall be born of a virgin;
> Christ should suffer under Pilate and at the hands of sinners;
> Christ should descend into hell and rise again the third day;
> Christ should ascend to the throne and reign forever at the right hand of the Majesty on High.
> THE DEATH OF CHRIST AT CALVARY IS THE MAINSPRING OF GOD'S DIVINE PREDESTINATION! And may I add, God does not predestinate men to hell! They're already headed there! He must stop their running from Him and turn them around to come to Him. That is the job of the Holy Spirit!

The Death of Christ Was Absolutely Necessary Because of the Law of God.

The law of God shows us the requirements of God's holiness. If men are going to Heaven, the law's demands must be met. BUT WHO CAN KEEP THE LAW AS GOD REQIRES IT? THE LAW REQUIRES PERFECTION!

The law required that the Priest had to be outwardly physically perfect, not a mole, not a scar, not one physical blemish on his body. A Pure and Perfect Priest had to offer a pure and Perfect Sacrifice with not one blemish!

GOD DEMANDS ABSOLUTE PURITY AND ABSOLUTE HOLINESS: The Scripture teaches us that to offend in just one point makes us guilty of all!

We cannot meet the requirements of the law; the demands of the law. The law curses the whole human race! Romans 6:23 "The wages of sin is death . . . ." Galatians 2:10 says "We must continue forever with no breaking point. No slowing down. No resting. 100% of the time awake or asleep- Absolute holiness, absolute righteousness, and absolute perfection. This means you can't even have a bad dream! IT REQUIRES 100% attention 100% of the time! in all things written in law," and we in no way have not continued to do all that the law demands.

IT IS THE LAW THAT SAYS "WITHOUT THE SHEDDING OF BLOOD THERE IS NO REMISSION OF SINS." <u>The law requires death and blood!</u>

But, Hallelujah, CHRIST SUFFERED THE PENALTY OF THE LAW FOR HIS PEOPLE! <u>He died and shed His blood, satisfying the demands of the law</u>! He was and is our perfect sacrifice.

The Death of Christ Was Absolutely Necessary Because of SIN!

Adam sinned as our federal head, and we are all now guilty, and are the recipients of the judgment of God passed upon Adam's sin.

> Sin separated man from the fellowship of God. Man therefore in His natural state is out of fellowship with God. WE ARE ABSOLUTELY, TOTALLY ALIENATED FROM GOD! AS FOREIGN TO GOD AS YOU ARE A RATTLESNAKE! In his natural, sinful state, man no longer delights to come into God's presence, but flees from God, and sews figs leaves of excuses. Man's desire is to hide himself from God as Adam hid in the garden. Why don't you like the power of the Holy God operating in you? Why don't you like old time religion? The spirit and voice of God constantly and consistently asks "Where art thou?" Men flee from that question. It exposes them! It makes them feel naked and ashamed!

The only way for God to restore fallen man back into fellowship with Him, to put away sin, and secure salvation; was to take on a robe of flesh, become a man, and in human form, meet the demands of God's justice!

Note!   <u>God Was Not Compelled to Save Man, But Rather Purposed to save him</u>.

Once God purposed to redeem sinners, He had to meet the demands of the law and shed blood in fact – <u>The Blood of the Lamb</u>!

The Lord was under no obligation to save a poor worm like me. I deserved hell, and Christ owed me nothing. PRAISE GOD, He saw me in my helpless condition, even before the world began <u>And He Loved Me</u>! Why? I cannot explain it! I do not know! But, somehow, known only to God, His heart beat for my redemption, and it pleased Him to take my sins upon Himself and bear them away as far as the East is from the West. He Chose Me to Salvation; Not the World – But <u>Me</u>! <u>Glory to God, it's personal.</u> He reconciled me to Himself. His Work at Calvary is Personal and Precious, And Because of Him I Am Free!

The Cross was No Accident! My Salvation was no surprise to God! My Sin Was Put in Hell on Calvary. Justice punished Sin, while Mercy was redeeming sinners!

> And It is <u>Finished</u>! Done! The Greek word for finished is the same Hebrew word for "Very Good!" in the Book of Genesis. When God said in His creation it was "Very Good," He was saying "IT IS FINISHED!", "IT <u>IS COMPLETE</u>!", "<u>IT IS DONE</u>!", ONCE AND FOR ALL! And on Calvary He was saying, "It's complete and it's very good!"

God is sovereign, and has a purpose in everything. Nothing takes God by surprise, and everything in His plan will take place as He planned it.

The words "chance" and "luck" should not be in the Christian's vocabulary.

There is no such thing to the child of God. Everything that happens to us is in the providence of God.

Calvary, and everything that was accomplished there was in the purpose and plan of God! The Purpose of Calvary is very clear.

"He shall save His people from their sins." Matthew 1:21
The Purpose of Calvary is Very Definite.
> He came to give eternal life to as many as God the Father had given Him. (John 6:37)
> There is a definite people for whom Christ died. They are known as "the church" or "the elect," and their names were written in the Lamb's Book of Life before the foundation of the world. The number in that book cannot be increased or decreased. It is a sealed Book, and no one knows the names therein except He who has written them! And He whom God the Holy Ghost has called by name! That sinner then can say,

"My name once stood with sinners, lost and bore a painful record. But by His blood the Savior crossed and placed it on His roll. I Know My Name Is There!"

The Purpose of Calvary is Very Specific
> Christ did not go to Calvary as a mere chance that Jesus took that someone, somewhere, someday, might believe on Him! No where in God's Word can you find such teaching as that!
> The Purpose of Calvary was to specifically save specific sinners! The Atonement of God is very specific.

Matthew 1:21 "He shall save – 'His People' from their sin!"
Christ has a people, has always had a people! He went to Calvary FOR THEM! FOR THEIR REDEMPTION!
The Purpose of Calvary is Very Successful
Everyone for Whom Christ Died Will Be in the Eternal Presence of God! He Will Not Now, nor has He ever lost one!
The Work of Calvary was a triumphant victory. The Son of God did not fail; the Holy Ghost does not fail! His people are being saved from their sin!
When the dust is settled and the smoke is cleared, when the final battle has been fought and won. Satan will not have anything that God wanted for Himself!

Let's now look at the Objects of the Benefits of Calvary!
> The Objects of Eternal Life are those whom the Father hath given the Son. (Read John 17:2, 6 and verses 9 through 11, and verse 24.) Jesus said, "I pray for them . . . that they be with me where I am. . . ." HAS THER EVER BEEN A PRAYER THAT JESUS PRAYED THAT GOD DID NOT HEAR AND ANSWER? HE'S ALREADY PRAYED ME INTO HEAVEN! HOW CAN I NOT MAKE IT? BECAUSE OF HIM, I'LL BE THERE!
> Before you violently declare God to be unfair and unjust, you must understand that you cannot appraise God's actions according to our depraved human standards!

The Benefits of the Old Rugged Cross are for the Children of God! Before you quibble and complain about God being unfair or unjust let me ask you a question: <u>When Christ Died Weren't There Already People in Hell? Well, did Christ die for them too?</u> And another thing, <u>Christ did not die for, and pay the sin debt for a sinner, then send him to hell to pay for it too!</u> That would really be unfair, for their sins are paid for twice!

You Can Be Sure of One Thing; Those Whom Christ Came to Redeem <u>Shall Be Redeemed!</u> All the forces of Hell cannot keep them out of Heaven.

Who Are They? The Bible Uses several different terms to describe them! <u>His People</u> – Matthew 1:21 "He shall save <u>His people</u> from their sins." Who are these people?

Those who were given to Christ in the Covenant of Grace before the foundation of the World!

And He said, "All that the Father giveth Me **shall** come to Me." John 6:37

And He said, ". . . of all that He hath given Me, I should lose nothing." John 6:39

Who are those for whom Christ died to Redeem?

<u>His Sheep</u> – John 10:15 "I lay down My life for the sheep."

Who are they?

<u>His Friends</u> – John 15:13 "Greater love hath no man than this that a man lay down his life for <u>his friends</u>."

Who are they?

<u>His Church</u> – Acts 20:28 ". . . Feed the Church of God which He hath purchased with His own blood!"

If the church is that important to Him, how important is it to you?

Who are they?

His Elect – Romans 8:33 "Who shall lay anything to the charge of God's elect."

1 Peter 1:2 ". . . elect according to the foreknowledge of God."

God Centers Everything Around Calvary and Around His Son!
1. The purposes of God's divine love are manifest in the cross.
2. The serpent's head is bruised <u>at the cross</u>.
3. The door of heaven is opened <u>at the cross</u>.
4. The resurrection was a completement <u>of the cross</u>!
5. All the great doctrines of grace revolve <u>Around the Cross</u>!
6. Our new life is born <u>at the cross</u>.
7. The world is stripped of its charm <u>at the Cross</u>!
8. Our condemnation is lifted <u>at the cross</u>.
9. The shadow of death is dispelled <u>at the cross</u>.
10. The heart of God is revealed <u>at the cross</u>!
11. I am saved <u>AT THE CROSS</u>!

I can only joy in the cross! Paul said, "But God forbid that I should glory, save in the cross of our Lord Jesus Christ!" Galatians 6:14

Christ's design in coming into this world and dying at Calvary was to accomplish something for a specific people – His chosen family! And not one of those He came to save shall ever perish in Hell!

Cursed by the law and bruised by the fall. Oh, the crimes I have committed against the divine law and nature of God. I need a sacrifice; I need a Savior! I need mercy. Is there a lamb for me? Is there one who would suffer for my sin? Yes, Oh Yes, I have found such a One AT THE CROSS!

AT THE CROSS
Alas! and did my Savior bleed
And did my Sov'reign die?
Would He devote that sacred head
For such a worm as I?
Was it for crimes that I had done
He groaned upon the tree?
Amazing pity! grace unknown!
And love beyond degree!

Chapter 9

Conclusion: A Final Thought About Our Redemption

Psalm 111:9
Hebrews 9:12
Colossians 1:12–21
Colossians 1:14
Hebrews 9:12
1 Peter 1:18–25
Ephesians 1:7
1 Corinthians 1:30

God hasn't stepped off the throne. He's the same yesterday, today, and forever. He's still God! His plan hasn't altered, His purpose hasn't been thwarted. In fact, He purposed in the council halls of eternal glory, before the foundation of the world to redeem Himself a people from Adam's fallen race; And in the midst of this sin cursed, God hating, hell bound world, God almighty is still redeeming men from sin! Our redemption goes far beyond even what our human minds can comprehend! Our redemption is the very handiwork of a Holy God. When you consider that He takes an old sinful, hellish, hell bound, ungodly man such as you and me, and in the operation of divine mercy and providence, reach in, and scoop us up out of the hell of this world, and wash us clean in Calvary's crimson flow. Kiss our sins away and make us new creatures like as unto the Son of God, head us eternally into a city foursquare with walls of Jasper, and streets of Gold where the lamb of God is the light thereof, and we'll enjoy the blessed glory of one eternal day with Christ our Savior, we can only say hallelujah for our redemption! We must look to Him our Redeemer and say it can only be grace! Wonderful, glorious, marvelous, amazing grace that forevermore redeemed us from the corruptible seed of Adam's race!

Redemption then is the workmanship of a Holy God!

Isn't it glorious that God has let us get in on some things that reaches far beyond the understanding of this world, and even reaches beyond the stars and the galaxies and reaches even beyond the understanding of Angels and into the world where God is!

We are a redeemed people; born again by the power of God. That friend, reaches beyond the boundaries of fallen man. God looked down and in mercy bestowed favor upon us, not because of works of righteousness which we had done, but in the holiness of His own sovereignty somehow chose not to pass us by! For reasons according to His own divine sovereign purpose, in His great plan of redemption He chose to span the great gulf of sin, and come to where you and I were, and with a finger of conviction, and an irresistible call of grace, redeem us from the mire of corruption!

The way of grace is not always easy. Sometimes it's rough and hard and a struggle. But you're headed for the mountaintop.

Illustration:

Climb to the top of a mountain. You'll go through rough, hard, rocky, steep, briars, and brambles, but reach the top and look back down upon where you just came from. The tree tops look like carpet, and it doesn't look near as rough as it did when you came through!

Oh we don't always see the handiwork of God as we come through, fighting the circum- stances, battling the storms, walking through the trials, but, Oh, when we hit the mountaintop, and God allows us to look down over the way, all you can see is the carpet of grace, and you say "My, it doesn't look near as bad as it did when I came through that situation." That's the operation of Heaven, the operation of grace, the operation of redemption in your soul!

God in His glory, God in His wisdom, God in His Power, saw fit to drop you down in the middle of all that He is, and teach you some things about Himself, His character, His grace, and His providence!

Hey, we don't have to drop our heads to anybody, we don't have to be downcast, we're God's children. We're walking out with Heaven in our bosom, and glory in our soul! Let the crowd say what they will; the grace of God in our soul will keep you walking on, and keep you pressing on, and when Hell is raging on every side, God's still running the show, and we'll hang onto Him! Hallelujah! He'll take us through to the other side!

We're redeemed! Redeemed!

I. The Price of Our Redemption

    A. Not with corruptible things such as silver and gold!

        1. Redemption –Not for Sale
        2. The gospel – Not for Sale
        3. God's preacher – Not for sale
            a. keep your salaries
            b. keep your big cars
            c. keep your fine parsonage
            d. keep your retirement, annuities, insurances, and any other benefits
            e. keep your associated prominence
            f. keep your pride, prestige, and position

The Gospel and God's man can't be bought off!
    Redemption: NOT FOR SALE!

    B. You Can't Buy Redemption With:

1. Pride	6. Church Membership	11. Bible Knowledge
2. Prestige	7. Political Position	12. Emotionalism
3. Popularity	8. Morality	13. Denominational
4. Baptism	9. Church Office	Position
5. Big Offering	10. Regular Church Attendance	

    C. Not By the Vain Conversation Received by the Tradition of Your Fathers!

        1. The foundation of Old Time Religion has been cast aside in their modern age for the vain conversation and traditions of men.

2. We have people in or churches today who claim to know God, claim to be redeemed (born again), but they live like hell and devil, their life and life-style is no different than it ever was. And when God's man begins to preach the separated lifestyle that is brought about by redemption, a changed life at Calvary, they get mad about it! They'd rather follow the traditions of men than the commands of God! Traditions of men will allow you to live, act, walk, talk, and dress any way you don't want to and still claim Christianity! We'd rather find a religion, a denomination, a church, a preacher, that will let us live like we please than to simply get right with God and be cleansed from our hellishness!

3. The crowd that claims to know God, but they care nothing about the things of God, care nothing about holiness and righteousness, and being filled with the Spirit, and getting on in and going with God. I doubt very seriously if they ever were born again!

4. Our denominations are full of it, and our churches are stinking with it! We don't want to hear it! We'll make every excuse in the book to hang onto our pet sins! We don't want to give up anything, and yet we want religion too!

5. Hey! Redemption will cause you to leave the world alone! Oddly, Separate yourself unto Christ! Live soberly, righteously, and Godly in Christ Jesus!

Romans 5:6-10
Luke 23:33
Galatians 1:3-5
1 Peter 1:18-21

II. We Are Saved by God's Grace by the Precious Blood!

1. We are living in the best educated society in human history.
2. A man can hardly preach anymore unless he's been to Bible School a year or two.
3. Education is fine, the means are there for everybody in these days, but the best education one can get is the school of God's Providence! And the school of God's grace!
   a. Sometimes your best education comes from getting back in the woods and bowing by an old stump and calling on God, or crawling around on your knees in the bedroom floor, crying out to almighty God, to move upon you; to get down in this old fashioned altar and beg God to fill you with the Holy Ghost!
4. This highly educated society denies everything God says is right! They've denied Calvary, the resurrection, the virgin birth, the atoning blood of Christ.
   a. This Bible, the founding principles of our church and our lives have been brought to an open shame by this modern society.
   b. But this modern society must realize, they're headed for hell at a dead run on a downhill grade! Our redemption (Salvation) is not from the popularity of this world but by the Precious Blood!
   c. Where are we Biblically? Why the spiritual decline of our people? And the "don't care" attitude displayed by today's generation?

5. Listen to me! After the death of all the Old Testament prophets, and the Holy Spirit departed, for 400 years between the pages of the Old and New Testaments there was no more prophecy. When there is no prophecy (No Prophets). (A preacher to say "Thus saith the Lord") The truths of revelation are neglected and despised! And the doctrines and traditions of men are preferred above the Word of God. That's where we are now!

    a. This period of time in the Scriptures spawned all manner and types of tradition and erroneous doctrines. This was the time when the sect of the Sadducees rose up. They were the "Free Thinkers" of their day. They didn't believe in Spiritual things at all. (No resurrection, no angels, no Spirit.) The Pharisees also spring up at this time and set up tradition as the rule of men's worship!

    b. But friends, Salvation is not received by the vain conversation. (Like the Sadducees) nor the tradition of men (Like the Pharisees), but by the Precious Blood of our Lord Jesus Christ!

6. Not One Drop Was Shed in Vain

    a. Every purpose God had in the shedding of the blood of Christ will be ultimately fulfilled!

    b. All man knows about it is the finite things BUT God Almighty's dealing at Calvary is an ETERNAL ISSUE!

7. AT CALVARY-
    God Almighty took eternity past in one hand, and eternity future in the other hand and tied the love knot of Grace!

    a. God Almighty made a path AT CALVARY for fallen ruined sinners to walk home in eternal redemption to be with God forevermore!

    b. God never has had but one way! It was blood in garden, blood throughout the pages of the Old Testament, Blood at Calvary, blood around the Throne of God. It's blood that washed the robes white and spotless of those saints around the throne shouting HALLELUJAH to the Lamb! God's one and only way for the redemption of men is BLOOD! BLOOD! BLOOD! Atoning, Blessed, Cleansing, Delivering, Eternal, Forgiving, Glorifying, Holy, Infallible, Justifying, Life-giving, Noble, Omniscient, Precious, Quickening, Royal, Sufficient, Transforming, Unspotted, Victorious, Wonderful BLOOD! BLOOD! BLOOD! Flowing down through eternity to flood my never dying soul, and wash away the guilt and sin of Adam's race and make me pure and spotless and allow me to stand before God a new creature. A Redeemed Soul by the Precious Blood of the Lamb!

JUST LIKE CHRIST, I STAND BEFORE GOD PERFECT, WHOLE AND CLEANSED!

IV. The Plan of Redemption (CALVARY)

    A. Who verily was foreordained before the foundation of the world!

        But that's not all –

        Thank God He was manifest! In these last times for you.

(1 Peter 1:20)

Thank God He revealed in my heart who He is! He was manifest to and for me! He came to me! He could have left me alone, but Glory to God He was manifest! Revealed!

Oh, He was manifest in the flesh in a manger in Bethlehem. And the very Angels of God sang and shouted – Glory to God in the Highest!

But He appeared to me; was manifest, revealed, to me, a sinner, unrighteous unholy undeserving! Hallelujah!

I say along with the Angels! Glory to God in the Highest!!! The Holy Ghost takes care of the Plan of Redemption.

V.   The Purpose of Redemption (CALVARY)

That Your Faith And Hope May Be In God!

This faith and hope creates and purposes perseverance! The divine call of God NEVER ceases! When you fall, He says, "GET UP SON – COME ON!"

Keep on Keepin' On

We're Redeemed! And One Day we'll be ushered into the eternal presence of God at home forever!

But until then – Lean on His bosom, Rest on His everlasting Arm. Cast all your care upon Him! He careth for you! Every time you need Him, HE WILL BE THERE!

And when you finally walk into God's Heaven, and stand before Him a finished product. You'll be like unto the Son of God and He'll say Welcome Home! Come in and Rest! And the Clouds of Glory in your soul will burst into everlasting Song, and Praise, and Hallelujahs- WORLD WITHOUT END!

AMEN

We're Redeemed!

We're Redeemed!

The Warrior's Prayer

Heavenly Father,
Your warrior prepares for battle.
Today I claim victory over Satan by putting on
the whole armor of God!

I put on the Girdle of Truth!
May I stand firm in the truth of Your Word
so I will not be a victim of Satan's lies.

I put on the Breastplate of Righteousness!
May it guard my heart from evil
so I will remain pure and holy,
protected under the blood of Jesus Christ.

I put on the Shoes of Peace!
May I stand firm in the Good News of the Gospel
so Your peace will shine through me
and be a light to all I encounter.

I take the Shield of Faith!
May I be ready for Satan's fiery darts of
doubt, denial and deceit
so I will not be vulnerable to spiritual defeat.

I put on the Helmet of Salvation!
May I keep my mind focused on You
so Satan will not have a stronghold on my
thoughts.

I take the Sword of the Spirit!
May the two-edged sword of Your Word
be ready in my hands
so I can expose the tempting words of Satan.

By faith your warrior has put on
the whole armor of God!

I am prepared to live this day in spiritual victory!

Amen

Scripture Index

All Scripture is taken from the King James Version Bible

<u>Preface</u>

Galatians 6:14

14 But God forbid that I should glory, save in the cross of our Lord Jesus Christ, by whom the world is crucified unto me, and I unto the world.

<u>Dedication</u>

2 Timothy 2:15

15 Study to shew thyself approved unto God, a workman that needeth not be ashamed, rightly dividing the word of truth.

<u>Special Annotation</u>

Proverbs 31:10–31

10 Who can find a virtuous woman? for her place is far above rubies.
11 The heart of her husband doth safely trust in her, so that he shall have no need of spoil.
12 She will do him good and not evil all the days of her life.
13 She seeketh wool, and flax, and worketh willingly with her hands.
14 She is like the merchants' ships; she bringeth her food from afar.
15 She riseth also while it is yet night, and giveth meat to her household, and a portion to her maidens.
16 She considereth a field, and buyeth it: with the fruit of her hands she planteth a vineyard.
17 She girdeth her loins with strength, and strengtheneth her arms.
18 She perceiveth that her merchandise is good; her candle goeth not out by night.
19 She layeth her hands to the spindle, and her hands hold the distaff.
20 She stretcheth out her hand to the poor; yea she reacheth forth her hands to the needy.
21 She is not afraid of the snow for her household: for all her household are clothed with scarlet.
22 She maketh herself coverings of tapestry; her clothing is silk and purple.
23 Her husband is known in the gates, when he sitteth among the elders of the land.
24 She maketh fine linen, and selleth it; and delivereth girdles unto the merchant.
25 Strength and honour are her clothing; and she shall rejoice in time to come.
26 She openeth her mouth with wisdom; and in her tongue is the law of kindness.
27 She looketh well to the ways of her household, and eateth not the bread of idleness.

28 Her children arise up, and call her blessed; her husband also, and he praiseth her.
29 Many daughters have done virtuously, but thou excelleth them all.
30 Favour is deceitful, and beauty is vain: but a woman that feareth the LORD, she shall be praised.
31 Give her of the fruit of her hands; and let her own works praise her in the gates.

Chapter One

1 Corinthians 11:17–30

17 Now in this that I declare unto you I praise you not, that ye come together not for the better, but for the worse.
18 For first of all, when ye come together in the church, I hear that there be divisions among you; and I partly believe it.
19 For there must be also heresies among you, that they which are approved may be made manifest among you.
20 When ye come together therefore into one place, this is not to eat the Lord's supper.
21 For in eating every one taketh before other his own supper: and one is hungry, and another is drunken.
22 What? have ye not houses to eat and to drink in? or despise ye the church of God, and shame them that have not? What shall I say to you? shall I praise you in this? I praise you not.
23 For I have received of the Lord that which also I delivered unto you, That the Lord Jesus the same night in which he was betrayed took bread:
24 And when he had given thanks, he brake it, and said, Take, eat: this is my body, which is broken for you: this do in remembrance of me.
25 After the same manner also he took the up, when he had supped, saying, This cup is the new testament in my blood: this do ye, as oft as ye drink it, in remembrance of me.
26 For as often as ye eat this bread, and drink this cup, ye do shew the Lord's death till he come.
27 Wherefore whosoever shall eat this bread, and drink this cup of the Lord, unworthily, shall be guilty of the body and blood of the Lord.
28 But let a man examine himself, and so let him eat of that bread, and drink of that cup.
29 For he that eateth and drinketh unworthily, eateth and drinketh damnation to himself, not discerning the Lord's body.
30 For this cause many are weak and sickly among you, and many sleep.

1 Corinthians 5:6–8

6 Your glorying is not good. Know ye not that a little leaven leaveneth the whole lump?
7 Purge out therefore the old leaven, that ye may be a new lump, as ye are unleavened. For even Christ our passover is sacrificed for us:
8 Therefore let us keep the feast, not with old leaven, neither with the leaven of malice and wickedness; but with the unleavened bread of sincerity and truth.

Matthew 26:18–29

18 And he said, Go into the city to such a man, and say unto him, The Master saith, My time is at hand; I will keep the passover at thy house with my disciples.
19 And the disciples did as Jesus had appointed them; and they made ready the passover.

20 Now when the even was come, he sat down with the twelve.

21 And as they did eat, he said, Verily I say unto you, that one of you shall betray me.

22 And they were exceedingly sorrowful, and began every one of them to say unto him, Lord, is it I?

23 And he answered and said, He that dippeth his hand with me in the dish, the same shall betray me.

24 The Son of man goeth as it is written of him: but woe unto that man by whom the Son of man is betrayed! it had been good for that man if he had not been born.

25 Then Judas, which betrayed him, answered and said, Master, is it I? He said unto him, Thou hast said.

26 And as they were eating Jesus took bread, and blessed it, and brake it, and gave it to the disciples, and said, Take, eat; this is my body.

27 And he took the cup, and gave thanks, and gave it to them, saying, Drink ye all of it;

28 For this is my blood of the new testament, which is shed for many for the remission of sins.

29 But I say unto you, I will not drink henceforth of this fruit of the vine, until that day when I drink it new with you in my Father's kingdom.

Exodus 12:1-14, 21-27

1 And the LORD spake unto Moses and Aaron in the land of Egypt saying,

2 This month shall be unto you the beginning of months: it shall be the first month of the year to you.

3 Speak ye unto all the congregation of Israel, saying, In the tenth day of this month they shall take to them every man a lamb, according to the house of their fathers, a lamb for an house:

4 And if the household be too little for the lamb, let him and his neighbor next unto his house take it according to the number of the souls; every man according to his eating shall make your count for the lamb.

5 Your lamb shall be without blemish, a male of the first year: ye shall take it out from the sheep, or from the goats:

6 And ye shall keep it up until the fourteenth day of the same month: and the whole assembly of the congregation of Israel shall kill it in the evening.

7 And they shall take of the blood, and strike it on the two side posts and on the upper door post of the houses, wherein they shall eat it.

8 And they shall eat the flesh in that night, roast with fire, and unleavened bread; and with bitter herbs they shall eat it.

9 Eat not of it raw, nor sodden at all with water, but roast with fire; his head with his legs, and with the purtenance thereof.

10 And ye shall let nothing of it remain until the morning; and that which remaineth of it until the morning ye shall burn with fire.

11 And thus shall ye eat it; with your loins girded, your shoes on your feet, and your staff in your hand; and ye shall eat it in haste: it is the LORD's passover.

12 For I will pass through the land of Egypt this night, and will smite all the firstborn in the land of Egypt, both man and beast; and against all the gods of Egypt I will execute judgment: I am the LORD.

13 And the blood shall be to you for a token upon the houses where ye are: and when I see the blood, I will pass over you, and the plague shall not be upon you to destroy you, when I smite the land of Egypt.

14 And this day shall be unto you for a memorial; and ye shall keep it a feast to the LORD throughout your generations; ye shall keep it a feast by an ordinance for ever.

21 Then Moses called for all the elders of Israel, and said unto them, Draw out and take you a lamb according to your families, and kill the passover.

22 And ye shall take a bunch of hyssop, and dip it in the blood that is in the bason, and strike the lintel and the two side posts with the blood that is in the bason; and none of you shall go out at the door of his house until the morning.

23 For the LORD will pass through to smite the Egyptians; and when he seeth the blood upon the lintel, and on the two side posts, the LORD will pass over the door, and will not suffer the destroyer to come in unto your houses to smite you.

24 And ye shall observe this thing for an ordinance to thee and to thy sons for ever.

25 And it shall come to pass, when ye be come to the land which the LORD will give you, according as he hath promised, that ye shall keep this service.

26 And it shall come to pass, when your children shall say unto you, What mean ye by this service?

27 That ye shall say, It is the sacrifice of the LORD's passover, who passed over the houses of the children of Israel in Egypt, when he smote the Egyptians, and delivered our houses. And the people bowed the head and worshipped.

Genesis 1:5

5 And God called the light Day, and the darkness he called Night. And the evening and the morning were the first day.

Exodus 12

1 And the LORD spake unto Moses and Aaron in the land of Egypt saying,

2 This month shall be unto you the beginning of months: it shall be the first month of the year to you.

3 Speak ye unto all the congregation of Israel, saying, In the tenth day of this month they shall take to them every man a lamb, according to the house of their fathers, a lamb for an house:

4 And if the household be too little for the lamb, let him and his neighbour next unto his house take it according to the number of the souls; every man according to his eating shall make your count for the lamb.

5 Your lamb shall be without blemish, a male of the first year: ye shall take it out from the sheep, or from the goats:

6 And ye shall keep it up until the fourteenth day of the same month: and the whole assembly of the congregation of Israel shall kill it in the evening.

7 And they shall take of the blood, and strike it on the two side posts and on the upper door post of the houses, wherein they shall eat it.

8 And they shall eat the flesh in that night, roast with fire, and unleavened bread; and with bitter herbs they shall eat it.

9 Eat not of it raw, nor sodden at all with water, but roast with fire; his head with his legs, and with the purtenance thereof.

10 And ye shall let nothing of it remain until the morning; and that which remaineth of it until the morning ye shall burn with fire.

11 And thus shall ye eat it; with your loins girded, your shoes on your feet, and your staff in your hand; and ye shall eat it in haste: it is the LORD's passover.

12 For I will pass through the land of Egypt this night, and will smite all the firstborn in the land of Egypt, both man and beast; and against all the gods of Egypt I will execute judgment: I am the LORD.

13 And the blood shall be to you for a token upon the houses where ye are: and when I see the blood, I will pass over you, and the plague shall not be upon you to destroy you, when I smite the land of Egypt.

14 And this day shall be unto you for a memorial; and ye shall keep it a feast to the LORD throughout your generations; ye shall keep it a feast by an ordinance for ever.

15 Seven days shall ye eat unleavened bread; even the first day ye shall put away leaven out of your houses: for whosoever eateth leavened bread from the first day until the seventh day, that soul shall be cut off from Israel.

16 And in the first day there shall be an holy convocation, and in the seventh day there shall be an holy convocation to you; no manner of work shall be done in them, save that which every man must eat, that only may be done of you.

17 And ye shall observe the feast of unleavened bread; for in this selfsame day have I brought your armies out of the land of Egypt: therefore shall ye observe this day in your generations by an ordinance for ever.

18 In the first month, on the fourteenth day of the month at even, ye shall eat unleavened bread, until the one and twentieth day of the month at even.

19 Seven days shall there be no leaven found in your houses: for whosoever eateth that which is leavened, even that soul shall be cut off from the congregation of Israel, whether he be a stranger, or born in the land.

20 Ye shall eat nothing leavened; in all your habitations shall ye eat unleavened bread.

21 Then Moses called for all the elders of Israel, and said unto them, Draw out and take you a lamb according to your families, and kill the passover.

22 And ye shall take a bunch of hyssop, and dip it in the blood that is in the bason, and strike the lintel and the two side posts with the blood that is in the bason; and none of you shall go out at the door of his house until the morning.

23 For the LORD will pass through to smite the Egyptians; and when he seeth the blood upon the lintel, and on the two side posts, the LORD will pass over the door, and will not suffer the destroyer to come in unto your houses to smite you.

24 And ye shall observe this thing for an ordinance to thee and to thy sons for ever.

25 And it shall come to pass, when ye be come to the land which the LORD will give you, according as he hath promised, that ye shall keep this service.

26 And it shall come to pass, when your children shall say unto you, What mean ye by this service?

27 That ye shall say, It is the sacrifice of the LORD's passover, who passed over the houses of the children of Israel in Egypt, when he smote the Egyptians, and delivered our houses. And the people bowed the head and worshipped.

28 And the children of Israel went away, and did as the LORD had commanded Moses and Aaron, so did they.

29 And it came to pass, that at midnight the LORD smote all the firstborn in the land of Egypt, from the firstborn of Pharaoh that sat on his throne unto the firstborn of the captive that was in the dungeon; and all the firstborn of cattle.

30 And Pharaoh rose up in the night, he, and all his servants, and all the Egyptians; and there was a great cry in Egypt; for there was not a house where there was not one dead.

31 And he called for Moses and Aaron by night, and said, Rise up, and get you forth from among my people, both ye and the children of Israel; and go, serve the LORD, as ye have said.

32 Also take your flocks and your herds, as ye have said, and be gone; and bless me also.

33 And the Egyptians were urgent upon the people, that they might send them out of the land in haste; for they said, We be all dead men.

34 And the people took their dough before it was leavened, their kneadingtroughs being bound up in their clothes upon their shoulders.

35 And the children of Israel did according to the word of Moses; and they borrowed of the Egyptians jewels of silver, and jewels of gold, and raiment:

36 And the LORD gave the people favour in the sight of the Egyptians, so that they lent unto them such things as they required. And they spoiled the Egyptians.

37 And the children of Israel journeyed from Rameses to Succoth, about six hundred thousand on foot that were men, beside children.

38 And a mixed multitude went up also with them; and flocks, and herds, even very much cattle.

39 And they baked unleavened cakes of the dough which they brought forth out of Egypt, for it was not leavened; because they were thrust out of Egypt, and could not tarry, neither had they prepared for themselves any victual.

40 Now the sojourning of the children of Israel, who dwelt in Egypt, was four hundred and thirty years.

41 And it came to pass at the end of the four hundred and thirty years, even the selfsame day it came to pass, that all the hosts of the LORD went out from the land of Egypt.

42 It is a night to be much observed unto the LORD for bringing them out from the land of Egypt: this is that night of the LORD to be observed of all the children of Israel in their generations.

43 And the LORD said unto Moses and Aaron, This is the ordinance of the passover: There shall no stranger eat thereof:

44 But every man's servant that is bought for money, when thou hast circumcised him, then shall he eat thereof.

45 A foreigner and an hired servant shall not eat thereof.

46 In one house shall it be eaten; thou shalt not carry forth ought of the flesh abroad out of the house; neither shall ye break a bone thereof.

47 All the congregation of Israel shall keep it.

48 And when a stranger shall sojourn with thee, and will keep the passover to the LORD, let all his males be circumcised, and then let him come near and keep it; and he shall be as one that is born in the land: for no uncircumcised person shall eat thereof.

49 One law shall be to him that is homeborn, and unto the stranger that sojourneth among you.

50 Thus did all the children of Israel; as the LORD commanded Moses and Aaron, so did they.

51 And it came to pass the selfsame day, that the LORD did bring the children of Israel out of the land of Egypt by their armies.

Exodus 12:24-27

24 And ye shall observe this thing for an ordinance to thee and to thy sons for ever.

25 And it shall come to pass, when ye be come to the land which the LORD will give you, according as he hath promised, that ye shall keep this service.

26 And it shall come to pass, when your children shall say unto you, What mean ye by this service?

27 That ye shall say, It is the sacrifice of the LORD's passover, who passed over the houses of the children of Israel in Egypt, when he smote the Egyptians, and delivered our houses. And the people bowed the head and worshipped by their armies.

Psalm 19:1

1 The heavens declare the glory of God; and the firmament sheweth his handiwork.

Ezekiel 8:14

14 Then he brought me to the door of the gate of the LORD's house which was toward the north; and, behold, there sat women weeping for Tammuz.

John 6:37

37 All that the Father giveth me shall come to me; and him that cometh to me I will in no wise cast out.

Exodus 34

1 And the LORD said unto Moses, Hew thee two tables of stone like unto the first: and I will write upon these tables the words that were in the first tables, which thou brakest.
2 And be ready in the morning, and come up in the morning unto mount Sinai, and present thyself there to me in the top of the mount.
3 And no man shall come up with thee, neither let any man be seen throughout all the mount; neither let the flocks nor herds feed before that mount.
4 And he hewed two tables of stone like unto the first; and Moses rose up early in the morning, and went up unto mount Sinai, as the LORD had commanded him, and took in his hand the two tables of stone.
5 And the LORD descended in the cloud, and stood with him there, and proclaimed the name of the LORD.
6 And the LORD passed by before him, and proclaimed, The LORD, The LORD God, merciful and gracious, longsuffering, and abundant in goodness and truth,
7 Keeping mercy for thousands, forgiving iniquity and transgression and sin, and that will by no means clear the guilty; visiting the iniquity of the fathers upon the children, and upon the children's children, unto the third and to the fourth generation.
8 And Moses made haste, and bowed his head toward the earth, and worshipped.
9 And he said, If now I have found grace in thy sight, O LORD, let my LORD, I pray thee, go among us; for it is a stiffnecked people; and pardon our iniquity and our sin, and take us for thine inheritance.
10 And he said, Behold, I make a covenant: before all thy people I will do marvels, such as have not been done in all the earth, nor in any nation: and all the people among which thou art shall see the work of the LORD: for it is a terrible thing that I will do with thee.
11 Observe thou that which I command thee this day: behold, I drive out before thee the Amorite, and the Canaanite, and the Hittite, and the Perizzite, and the Hivite, and the Jebusite.
12 Take heed to thyself, lest thou make a covenant with the inhabitants of the land whither thou goest, lest it be for a snare in the midst of thee:
13 But ye shall destroy their altars, break their images, and cut down their groves:
14 For thou shalt worship no other god: for the LORD, whose name is Jealous, is a jealous God:
15 Lest thou make a covenant with the inhabitants of the land, and they go a whoring after their gods, and do sacrifice unto their gods, and one call thee, and thou eat of his sacrifice;
16 And thou take of their daughters unto thy sons, and their daughters go a whoring after their gods, and make thy sons go a whoring after their gods.
17 Thou shalt make thee no molten gods.
18 The feast of unleavened bread shalt thou keep. Seven days thou shalt eat unleavened bread, as I commanded thee, in the time of the month Abib: for in the month Abib thou camest out from Egypt.

19 All that openeth the matrix is mine; and every firstling among thy cattle, whether ox or sheep, that is male.

20 But the firstling of an ass thou shalt redeem with a lamb: and if thou redeem him not, then shalt thou break his neck. All the firstborn of thy sons thou shalt redeem. And none shall appear before me empty.

21 Six days thou shalt work, but on the seventh day thou shalt rest: in earing time and in harvest thou shalt rest.

22 And thou shalt observe the feast of weeks, of the firstfruits of wheat harvest, and the feast of ingathering at the year's end.

23 Thrice in the year shall all your menchildren appear before the Lord God, the God of Israel.

24 For I will cast out the nations before thee, and enlarge thy borders: neither shall any man desire thy land, when thou shalt go up to appear before the Lord thy God thrice in the year.

25 Thou shalt not offer the blood of my sacrifice with leaven; neither shall the sacrifice of the feast of the passover be left unto the morning.

26 The first of the firstfruits of thy land thou shalt bring unto the house of the Lord thy God. Thou shalt not seethe a kid in his mother's milk.

27 And the Lord said unto Moses, Write thou these words: for after the tenor of these words I have made a covenant with thee and with Israel.

28 And he was there with the Lord forty days and forty nights; he did neither eat bread, nor drink water. And he wrote upon the tables the words of the covenant, the ten commandments.

29 And it came to pass, when Moses came down from mount Sinai with the two tables of testimony in Moses' hand, when he came down from the mount, that Moses wist not that the skin of his face shone while he talked with him.

30 And when Aaron and all the children of Israel saw Moses, behold, the skin of his face shone; and they were afraid to come nigh him.

31 And Moses called unto them; and Aaron and all the rulers of the congregation returned unto him: and Moses talked with them.

32 And afterward all the children of Israel came nigh: and he gave them in commandment all that the Lord had spoken with him in mount Sinai.

33 And till Moses had done speaking with them, he put a vail on his face.

34 But when Moses went in before the Lord to speak with him, he took the vail off, until he came out. And he came out, and spake unto the children of Israel that which he was commanded.

35 And the children of Israel saw the face of Moses, that the skin of Moses' face shone: and Moses put the vail upon his face again, until he went in to speak with him.

Romans 3

1 What advantage then hath the Jew? or what profit is there of circumcision?

2 Much every way: chiefly, because that unto them were committed the oracles of God.

3 For what if some did not believe? shall their unbelief make the faith of God without effect?

4 God forbid: yea, let God be true, but every man a liar; as it is written, That thou mightest be justified in thy sayings, and mightest overcome when thou art judged.

5 But if our unrighteousness commend the righteousness of God, what shall we say? Is God unrighteous who taketh vengeance? (I speak as a man)

6 God forbid: for then how shall God judge the world?

7 For if the truth of God hath more abounded through my lie unto his glory; why yet am I also judged as a sinner?

8 And not rather, (as we be slanderously reported, and as some affirm that we say,) Let us do evil, that good may come? whose damnation is just.

9 What then? are we better than they? No, in no wise: for we have before proved both Jews and Gentiles, that they are all under sin;

10 As it is written, There is none righteous, no, not one:

11 There is none that understandeth, there is none that seeketh after God.

12 They are all gone out of the way, they are together become unprofitable; there is none that doeth good, no, not one.

13 Their throat is an open sepulchre; with their tongues they have used deceit; the poison of asps is under their lips:

14 Whose mouth is full of cursing and bitterness:

15 Their feet are swift to shed blood:

16 Destruction and misery are in their ways:

17 And the way of peace have they not known:

18 There is no fear of God before their eyes.

19 Now we know that what things soever the law saith, it saith to them who are under the law: that every mouth may be stopped, and all the world may become guilty before God.

20 Therefore by the deeds of the law there shall no flesh be justified in his sight: for by the law is the knowledge of sin.

21 But now the righteousness of God without the law is manifested, being witnessed by the law and the prophets;

22 Even the righteousness of God which is by faith of Jesus Christ unto all and upon all them that believe: for there is no difference:

23 For all have sinned, and come short of the glory of God;

24 Being justified freely by his grace through the redemption that is in Christ Jesus:

25 Whom God hath set forth to be a propitiation through faith in his blood, to declare his righteousness for the remission of sins that are past, through the forbearance of God;

26 To declare, I say, at this time his righteousness: that he might be just, and the justifier of him which believeth in Jesus.

27 Where is boasting then? It is excluded. By what law? of works? Nay: but by the law of faith.

28 Therefore we conclude that a man is justified by faith without the deeds of the law.

29 Is he the God of the Jews only? is he not also of the Gentiles? Yes, of the Gentiles also:

30 Seeing it is one God, which shall justify the circumcision by faith, and uncircumcision through faith.

31 Do we then make void the law through faith? God forbid: yea, we establish the law.

Chapter 2

1 Corinthians 11:23-27

23 But we preach Christ crucified, unto the Jews a stumblingblock, and unto the Greeks foolishness;

24 But unto them which are called, both Jews and Greeks, Christ the power of God, and the wisdom of God.

25 Because the foolishness of God is wiser than men; and the weakness of God is stronger than men.

26 For ye see your calling, brethren, how that not many wise men after the flesh, not many mighty, not many noble, *are called*:

27 But God hath chosen the foolish things of the world to confound the wise; and God hath chosen the weak things of the world to confound the things which are mighty;

Exodus 12

1 And the LORD spake unto Moses and Aaron in the land of Egypt saying,

2 This month shall be unto you the beginning of months: it shall be the first month of the year to you.

3 Speak ye unto all the congregation of Israel, saying, In the tenth day of this month they shall take to them every man a lamb, according to the house of their fathers, a lamb for an house:

4 And if the household be too little for the lamb, let him and his neighbour next unto his house take it according to the number of the souls; every man according to his eating shall make your count for the lamb.

5 Your lamb shall be without blemish, a male of the first year: ye shall take it out from the sheep, or from the goats:

6 And ye shall keep it up until the fourteenth day of the same month: and the whole assembly of the congregation of Israel shall kill it in the evening.

7 And they shall take of the blood, and strike it on the two side posts and on the upper door post of the houses, wherein they shall eat it.

8 And they shall eat the flesh in that night, roast with fire, and unleavened bread; and with bitter herbs they shall eat it.

9 Eat not of it raw, nor sodden at all with water, but roast with fire; his head with his legs, and with the purtenance thereof.

10 And ye shall let nothing of it remain until the morning; and that which remaineth of it until the morning ye shall burn with fire.

11 And thus shall ye eat it; with your loins girded, your shoes on your feet, and your staff in your hand; and ye shall eat it in haste: it is the LORD's passover.

12 For I will pass through the land of Egypt this night, and will smite all the firstborn in the land of Egypt, both man and beast; and against all the gods of Egypt I will execute judgment: I am the LORD.

13 And the blood shall be to you for a token upon the houses where ye are: and when I see the blood, I will pass over you, and the plague shall not be upon you to destroy you, when I smite the land of Egypt.

14 And this day shall be unto you for a memorial; and ye shall keep it a feast to the LORD throughout your generations; ye shall keep it a feast by an ordinance for ever.

15 Seven days shall ye eat unleavened bread; even the first day ye shall put away leaven out of your houses: for whosoever eateth leavened bread from the first day until the seventh day, that soul shall be cut off from Israel.

16 And in the first day there shall be an holy convocation, and in the seventh day there shall be an holy convocation to you; no manner of work shall be done in them, save that which every man must eat, that only may be done of you.

17 And ye shall observe the feast of unleavened bread; for in this selfsame day have I brought your armies out of the land of Egypt: therefore shall ye observe this day in your generations by an ordinance for ever.

18 In the first month, on the fourteenth day of the month at even, ye shall eat unleavened bread, until the one and twentieth day of the month at even.

19 Seven days shall there be no leaven found in your houses: for whosoever eateth that which is leavened, even that soul shall be cut off from the congregation of Israel, whether he be a stranger, or born in the land.

20 Ye shall eat nothing leavened; in all your habitations shall ye eat unleavened bread.

21 Then Moses called for all the elders of Israel, and said unto them, Draw out and take you a lamb according to your families, and kill the passover.

22 And ye shall take a bunch of hyssop, and dip it in the blood that is in the bason, and strike the lintel and the two side posts with the blood that is in the bason; and none of you shall go out at the door of his house until the morning.

23 For the LORD will pass through to smite the Egyptians; and when he seeth the blood upon the lintel, and on the two side posts, the LORD will pass over the door, and will not suffer the destroyer to come in unto your houses to smite you.

24 And ye shall observe this thing for an ordinance to thee and to thy sons for ever.

25 And it shall come to pass, when ye be come to the land which the LORD will give you, according as he hath promised, that ye shall keep this service.

26 And it shall come to pass, when your children shall say unto you, What mean ye by this service?

27 That ye shall say, It is the sacrifice of the LORD's passover, who passed over the houses of the children of Israel in Egypt, when he smote the Egyptians, and delivered our houses. And the people bowed the head and worshipped.

28 And the children of Israel went away, and did as the LORD had commanded Moses and Aaron, so did they.

29 And it came to pass, that at midnight the LORD smote all the firstborn in the land of Egypt, from the firstborn of Pharaoh that sat on his throne unto the firstborn of the captive that was in the dungeon; and all the firstborn of cattle.

30 And Pharaoh rose up in the night, he, and all his servants, and all the Egyptians; and there was a great cry in Egypt; for there was not a house where there was not one dead.

31 And he called for Moses and Aaron by night, and said, Rise up, and get you forth from among my people, both ye and the children of Israel; and go, serve the LORD, as ye have said.

32 Also take your flocks and your herds, as ye have said, and be gone; and bless me also.

33 And the Egyptians were urgent upon the people, that they might send them out of the land in haste; for they said, We be all dead men.

34 And the people took their dough before it was leavened, their kneadingtroughs being bound up in their clothes upon their shoulders.

35 And the children of Israel did according to the word of Moses; and they borrowed of the Egyptians jewels of silver, and jewels of gold, and raiment:

36 And the LORD gave the people favour in the sight of the Egyptians, so that they lent unto them such things as they required. And they spoiled the Egyptians.

37 And the children of Israel journeyed from Rameses to Succoth, about six hundred thousand on foot that were men, beside children.

38 And a mixed multitude went up also with them; and flocks, and herds, even very much cattle.

39 And they baked unleavened cakes of the dough which they brought forth out of Egypt, for it was not leavened; because they were thrust out of Egypt, and could not tarry, neither had they prepared for themselves any victual.

40 Now the sojourning of the children of Israel, who dwelt in Egypt, was four hundred and thirty years.

41 And it came to pass at the end of the four hundred and thirty years, even the selfsame day it came to pass, that all the hosts of the LORD went out from the land of Egypt.

42 It is a night to be much observed unto the LORD for bringing them out from the land of Egypt: this is that night of the LORD to be observed of all the children of Israel in their generations.

43 And the LORD said unto Moses and Aaron, This is the ordinance of the passover: There shall no stranger eat thereof:

44 But every man's servant that is bought for money, when thou hast circumcised him, then shall he eat thereof.

45 A foreigner and an hired servant shall not eat thereof.

46 In one house shall it be eaten; thou shalt not carry forth ought of the flesh abroad out of the house; neither shall ye break a bone thereof.

47 All the congregation of Israel shall keep it.

48 And when a stranger shall sojourn with thee, and will keep the passover to the LORD, let all his males be circumcised, and then let him come near and keep it; and he shall be as one that is born in the land: for no uncircumcised person shall eat thereof.

49 One law shall be to him that is homeborn, and unto the stranger that sojourneth among you.

50 Thus did all the children of Israel; as the LORD commanded Moses and Aaron, so did they.

51 And it came to pass the selfsame day, that the LORD did bring the children of Israel out of the land of Egypt by their armies.

Matthew 26:18-29

18 And he said, Go into the city to such a man, and say unto him, The Master saith, My time is at hand; I will keep the passover at thy house with my disciples.

19 And the disciples did as Jesus had appointed them; and they made ready the passover.

20 Now when the even was come, he sat down with the twelve.

21 And as they did eat, he said, Verily I say unto you, that one of you shall betray me.

22 And they were exceeding sorrowful, and began every one of them to say unto him, Lord, is it I?

23 And he answered and said, He that dippeth his hand with me in the dish, the same shall betray me.

24 The Son of man goeth as it is written of him: but woe unto that man by whom the Son of man is betrayed! it had been good for that man if he had not been born.

25 Then Judas, which betrayed him, answered and said, Master, is it I? He said unto him, Thou has said.

26 And as they were eating, Jesus took bread, and blessed it, and brake it, and gave it to the disciples, and said, Take, eat; this is my body.

27 And he took the cup, and gave thanks, and gave it to them, saying, Drink ye all of it;

28 For this is my blood of the new testament, which is shed for the remission of sins.

Exodus 12 (See Chapter One above)

John 10:9

9 I am the door: by me if any man enter in, he shall be saved, and shall go in and out, and find pasture.

Hebrews 12:2

2 Looking unto Jesus the author and finisher of our faith; who for the joy that was set before him endured the cross, despising the shame, and is set down at the right hand of the throne of God.

1 Corinthians 11:23-24

23 For I have received of the Lord that which also I delivered unto you, that the Lord Jesus the same night in which he was betrayed took bread:

24 And when he had given thanks, he brake it, and said, Take, eat: this is my body, which is broken for you: this do in remembrance of me.

Exodus 12:21-27

21 Then Moses called for all the elders of Israel, and said unto them, Draw out and take you a lamb according to your families, and kill the passover.
22 And ye shall take a bunch of hyssop, and dip it in the blood that is in the bason, and strike the lintel and the two side posts with the blood that is in the bason; and none of you shall go out at the door of his house until the morning.
23 For the LORD will pass through to smite the Egyptians; and when he seeth the blood upon the lintel, and on the two side posts, the LORD will pass over the door, and will not suffer the destroyer to come in unto your houses to smite you.
24 And ye shall observe this thing for an ordinance to thee and to thy sons for ever.
25 And it shall come to pass, when ye be come to the land which the LORD will give you, according as he hath promised, that ye shall keep this service.
26 And it shall come to pass, when your children shall say unto you, What mean ye by this service?
27 That ye shall say, It is the sacrifice of the LORD's passover, who passed over the houses of the children of Israel in Egypt, when he smote the Egyptians, and delivered our houses. And the people bowed the head and worshipped.

Isaiah 64:6

6 But we are all as an unclean thing, and all our righteousness are as filthy rags; and we all do fade as a leaf; and our iniquities, like the wind, have taken us away.

Chapter 3

Isaiah 53:4-7, 10-11

4 Surely he hath borne our griefs, and carried our sorrows: yet we did esteem him stricken, smitten of God, and afflicted.
5 But he was wounded for our transgressions, he was bruised for our iniquities: the chastisement of our peace was upon him; and with his stripes we are healed.
6 All we like sheep have gone astray; we have turned every one to his own way; and the LORD hath laid on him the iniquity of us all.
7 He was oppressed, and he was afflicted, yet he opened not his mouth: he is brought as a lamb to the slaughter, and as a sheep before her shearers is dumb, so he openeth not his mouth.
10 Yet it pleased the LORD to bruise him; he hath put him to grief: when thou shalt make his soul an offering for sin, he shall see his seed, he shall prolong his days, and the pleasure of the LORD shall prosper in his hand.
11 He shall see of the travail of his soul, and shall be satisfied: by his knowledge shall my righteous servant justify many; for he shall bear their iniquities.

Matthew 26:36-46

36 Then cometh Jesus with them unto a place called Gethsemane, and saith unto the disciples, Sit ye here, while I go and pray yonder.
37 And he took with him Peter and the two sons of Zebedee, and began to be sorrowful and very heavy.
38 Then saith he unto them, My soul is exceeding sorrowful, even unto death: tarry ye here, and watch with me.
39 And he went a little farther, and fell on his face, and prayed, saying, O my Father, if it be possible, let this cup pass from me: nevertheless not as I will, but as thou wilt.
40 And he cometh unto the disciples, and findeth them asleep, and saith unto Peter, What, could ye not watch with me one hour?
41 Watch and pray, that ye enter not into temptation: the spirit indeed is willing, but the flesh is weak.
42 He went away again the second time, and prayed, saying, O my Father, if this cup may not pass away from me, except I drink it, thy will be done.
43 And he came and found them asleep again: for their eyes were heavy.
44 And he left them, and went away again, and prayed the third time, saying the same words.
45 Then cometh he to his disciples, and saith unto them, Sleep on now, and take your rest: behold, the hour is at hand, and the Son of man is betrayed into the hands of sinners.
46 Rise, let us be going: behold, he is at hand that doth betray me.

Hebrews 5:7-9

7 Who in the days of his flesh, when he had offered up prayers and supplications with strong crying and tears unto him that was able to save him from death, and was heard in that he feared;
8 Though he were a Son, yet learned he obedience by the things which he suffered;
9 And being made perfect, he became the author of eternal salvation unto all them that obey him;

John 12:27

27 Now is my soul troubled; and what shall I say? Father, save me from this hour: but for this cause came I unto this hour.

Matthew 26:37

37 And he took with him Peter and the two sons of Zebedee, and began to be sorrowful and very heavy.

Hebrews 12:21

21 And so terrible was the sight, that Moses said, I exceedingly fear and quake:

John 14:30

30 Hereafter I will not talk much with you: for the prince of this world cometh, and hath nothing in me.

Luke 22:53

53 When I was daily with you in the temple, ye stretched forth no hands against me: but this is your hour, and the power of darkness.

Genesis 1:2

2 And the earth was without form, and void; and darkness was upon the face of the deep. And the Spirit of God moved upon the face of the waters.

Hebrews 12:4

4 Ye have not yet resisted unto blood, striving against sin.

Hebrews 5:7

7 Who in the days of his flesh, when he had offered up prayers and supplications with strong crying and tears unto him that was able to save him from death, and was heard in that he feared.

Luke 22:44

44 And being in an agony he prayed more earnestly: and his sweat was as it were great drops of blood falling down to the ground.

Hebrews 5:7 (See above)

Acts 8:33

33 In his humiliation his judgment was taken away: and who shall declare his generation? for his life is taken from the earth.

Hebrews 2:17-18

17 Wherefore in all things it behoved him to be made like unto his brethren, that he might be a merciful and faithful high priest in things pertaining to God, to make reconciliation for the sins of the people.
18 For in that he himself hath suffered being tempted, he is able to succour them that are tempted.

Chapter 4

Isaiah 53:3

3 He is despised and rejected of men; a man of sorrows, and acquainted with grief: and we hid as it were our faces from him; he was despised, and we esteemed him not.

John 13:31-38

31 Therefore, when he was gone out, Jesus said, Now is the Son of man glorified, and God is glorified in him.
32 If God be glorified in him, God shall also glorify him in himself, and shall straightway glorify him.
33 Little children, yet a little while I am with you. Ye shall seek me: and as I said unto the Jews, Whither I go, ye cannot come; so now I say to you.
34 A new commandment I give unto you, That ye love one another; as I have loved you, that ye also love one another.
35 By this shall all men know that ye are my disciples, if ye have love one to another.
36 Simon Peter said unto him, Lord, whither goest thou? Jesus answered him, Whither I go, thou canst not follow me now; but thou shalt follow me afterwards.
37 Peter said unto him, Lord, why cannot I follow thee now? I will lay down my life for thy sake.
38 Jesus answered him, Wilt thou lay down thy life for my sake? Verily, verily, I say unto thee, The cock shall not crow, till thou hast denied me thrice.

Luke 10:25-37

25 And, behold, a certain lawyer stood up, and tempted him, saying, Master, what shall I do to inherit eternal life?
26 He said unto him, What is written in the law? how readest thou?
27 And he answering said, Thou shalt love the Lord thy God with all thy heart, and with all thy soul, and with all thy strength, and with all thy mind; and thy neighbour as thyself.
28 And he said unto him, Thou hast answered right: this do, and thou shalt live.
29 But he, willing to justify himself, said unto Jesus, And who is my neighbour?
30 And Jesus answering said, A certain man went down from Jerusalem to Jericho, and fell among thieves, which stripped him of his raiment, and wounded him, and departed, leaving him half dead.
31 And by chance there came down a certain priest that way: and when he saw him, he passed by on the other side.
32 And likewise a Levite, when he was at the place, came and looked on him, and passed by on the other side.
33 But a certain Samaritan, as he journeyed, came where he was: and when he saw him, he had compassion on him,
34 And went to him, and bound up his wounds, pouring in oil and wine, and set him on his own beast, and brought him to an inn, and took care of him.
35 And on the morrow when he departed, he took out two pence, and gave them to the host, and said unto him, Take care of him; and whatsoever thou spendest more, when I come again, I will repay thee.
36 Which now of these three, thinkest thou, was neighbour unto him that fell among the thieves?
37 And he said, He that shewed mercy on him. Then said Jesus unto him, Go, and do thou likewise.

Luke 23:13-25

13 And Pilate, when he had called together the chief priests and the rulers and the people,

14 Said unto them, Ye have brought this man unto me, as one that perverteth the people: and, behold, I, having examined him before you, have found no fault in this man touching those things whereof ye accuse him:

15 No, nor yet Herod: for I sent you to him; and, lo, nothing worthy of death is done unto him.

16 I will therefore chastise him, and release him.

17 (For of necessity he must release one unto them at the feast.)

18 And they cried out all at once, saying, Away with this man, and release unto us Barabbas:

19 (Who for a certain sedition made in the city, and for murder, was cast into prison.)

20 Pilate therefore, willing to release Jesus, spake again to them.

21 But they cried, saying, Crucify him, crucify him.

22 And he said unto them the third time, Why, what evil hath he done? I have found no cause of death in him: I will therefore chastise him, and let him go.

23 And they were instant with loud voices, requiring that he might be crucified. And the voices of them and of the chief priests prevailed.

24 And Pilate gave sentence that it should be as they required.

25 And he released unto them him that for sedition and murder was cast into prison, whom they had desired; but he delivered Jesus to their will.

John 19:1-6

1 Then Pilate therefore took Jesus, and scourged him.

2 And the soldiers platted a crown of thorns, and put it on his head, and they put on him a purple robe,

3 And said, Hail, King of the Jews! and they smote him with their hands.

4 Pilate therefore went forth again, and saith unto them, Behold, I bring him forth to you, that ye may know that I find no fault in him.

5 Then came Jesus forth, wearing the crown of thorns, and the purple robe. And Pilate saith unto them, Behold the man!

6 When the chief priests therefore and officers saw him, they cried out, saying, Crucify him, crucify him. Pilate saith unto them, Take ye him, and crucify him: for I find no fault in him.

Isaiah 50:6-7

6 I gave my back to the smiters, and my cheeks to them that plucked off the hair: I hid not my face from shame and spitting.

7 For the Lord God will help me; therefore shall I not be confounded: therefore have I set my face like a flint, and I know that I shall not be ashamed.

Isaiah 53:3-11

3 He is despised and rejected of men; a man of sorrows, and acquainted with grief: and we hid as it were our faces from him; he was despised, and we esteemed him not.

4 Surely he hath borne our griefs, and carried our sorrows: yet we did esteem him stricken, smitten of God, and afflicted.

5 But he was wounded for our transgressions, he was bruised for our iniquities: the chastisement of our peace was upon him; and with his stripes we are healed.

6 All we like sheep have gone astray; we have turned every one to his own way; and the LORD hath laid on him the iniquity of us all.

7 He was oppressed, and he was afflicted, yet he opened not his mouth: he is brought as a lamb to the slaughter, and as a sheep before her shearers is dumb, so he openeth not his mouth.

8 He was taken from prison and from judgment: and who shall declare his generation? for he was cut off out of the land of the living: for the transgression of my people was he stricken.

9 And he made his grave with the wicked, and with the rich in his death; because he had done no violence, neither was any deceit in his mouth.

10 Yet it pleased the Lord to bruise him; he hath put him to grief: when thou shalt make his soul an offering for sin, he shall see his seed, he shall prolong his days, and the pleasure of the Lord shall prosper in his hand.

11 He shall see of the travail of his soul, and shall be satisfied: by his knowledge shall my righteous servant justify many; for he shall bear their iniquities.

Revelation 19:1-5

1 And after these things I heard a great voice of much people in heaven, saying, Alleluia; Salvation, and glory, and honour, and power, unto the Lord our God:

2 For true and righteous are his judgments: for he hath judged the great whore, which did corrupt the earth with her fornication, and hath avenged the blood of his servants at her hand.

3 And again they said, Alleluia And her smoke rose up for ever and ever.

4 And the four and twenty elders and the four beasts fell down and worshipped God that sat on the throne, saying, Amen; Alleluia.

5 And a voice came out of the throne, saying, Praise our God, all ye his servants, and ye that fear him, both small and great.

Chapter 5

Matthew 27:45

45 Now from the sixth hour there was darkness over all the land unto the ninth hour.

John 19:19-27

19 And Pilate wrote a title, and put it on the cross. And the writing was Jesus Of Nazareth The King Of The Jews.

20 This title then read many of the Jews: for the place where Jesus was crucified was nigh to the city: and it was written in Hebrew, and Greek, and Latin.

21 Then said the chief priests of the Jews to Pilate, Write not, The King of the Jews; but that he said, I am King of the Jews.

22 Pilate answered, What I have written I have written.

23 Then the soldiers, when they had crucified Jesus, took his garments, and made four parts, to every soldier a part; and also his coat: now the coat was without seam, woven from the top throughout.

24 They said therefore among themselves, Let us not rend it, but cast lots for it, whose it shall be: that the scripture might be fulfilled, which saith, They parted my raiment among them, and for my vesture they did cast lots. These things therefore the soldiers did.

25 Now there stood by the cross of Jesus his mother, and his mother's sister, Mary the wife of Cleophas, and Mary Magdalene.

26 When Jesus therefore saw his mother, and the disciple standing by, whom he loved, he saith unto his mother, Woman, behold thy son!
27 Then saith he to the disciple, Behold thy mother! And from that hour that disciple took her unto his own home.

Luke 23:44-45

44 And it was about the sixth hour, and there was a darkness over all the earth until the ninth hour.
45 And the sun was darkened, and the veil of the temple was rent in the midst.

Exodus 10

1 And the Lord said unto Moses, Go in unto Pharaoh: for I have hardened his heart, and the heart of his servants, that I might shew these my signs before him:
2 And that thou mayest tell in the ears of thy son, and of thy son's son, what things I have wrought in Egypt, and my signs which I have done among them; that ye may know how that I am the Lord.
3 And Moses and Aaron came in unto Pharaoh, and said unto him, Thus saith the Lord God of the Hebrews, How long wilt thou refuse to humble thyself before me? let my people go, that they may serve me.
4 Else, if thou refuse to let my people go, behold, tomorrow will I bring the locusts into thy coast:
5 And they shall cover the face of the earth, that one cannot be able to see the earth: and they shall eat the residue of that which is escaped, which remaineth unto you from the hail, and shall eat every tree which groweth for you out of the field:
6 And they shall fill thy houses, and the houses of all thy servants, and the houses of all the Egyptians; which neither thy fathers, nor thy fathers' fathers have seen, since the day that they were upon the earth unto this day. And he turned himself, and went out from Pharaoh.
7 And Pharaoh's servants said unto him, How long shall this man be a snare unto us? let the men go, that they may serve the Lord their God: knowest thou not yet that Egypt is destroyed?
8 And Moses and Aaron were brought again unto Pharaoh: and he said unto them, Go, serve the Lord your God: but who are they that shall go?
9 And Moses said, We will go with our young and with our old, with our sons and with our daughters, with our flocks and with our herds will we go; for we must hold a feast unto the Lord.
10 And he said unto them, Let the Lord be so with you, as I will let you go, and your little ones: look to it; for evil is before you.
11 Not so: go now ye that are men, and serve the Lord; for that ye did desire. And they were driven out from Pharaoh's presence.
12 And the Lord said unto Moses, Stretch out thine hand over the land of Egypt for the locusts, that they may come up upon the land of Egypt, and eat every herb of the land, even all that the hail hath left.
13 And Moses stretched forth his rod over the land of Egypt, and the Lord brought an east wind upon the land all that day, and all that night; and when it was morning, the east wind brought the locusts.
14 And the locust went up over all the land of Egypt, and rested in all the coasts of Egypt: very grievous were they; before them there were no such locusts as they, neither after them shall be such.
15 For they covered the face of the whole earth, so that the land was darkened; and they did eat every herb of the land, and all the fruit of the trees which the hail had left: and there

remained not any green thing in the trees, or in the herbs of the field, through all the land of Egypt.

16 Then Pharaoh called for Moses and Aaron in haste; and he said, I have sinned against the Lord your God, and against you.

17 Now therefore forgive, I pray thee, my sin only this once, and intreat the Lord your God, that he may take away from me this death only.

18 And he went out from Pharaoh, and intreated the Lord.

19 And the Lord turned a mighty strong west wind, which took away the locusts, and cast them into the Red sea; there remained not one locust in all the coasts of Egypt.

20 But the Lord hardened Pharaoh's heart, so that he would not let the children of Israel go.

21 And the Lord said unto Moses, Stretch out thine hand toward heaven, that there may be darkness over the land of Egypt, even darkness which may be felt.

22 And Moses stretched forth his hand toward heaven; and there was a thick darkness in all the land of Egypt three days:

23 They saw not one another, neither rose any from his place for three days: but all the children of Israel had light in their dwellings.

24 And Pharaoh called unto Moses, and said, Go ye, serve the Lord; only let your flocks and your herds be stayed: let your little ones also go with you.

25 And Moses said, Thou must give us also sacrifices and burnt offerings, that we may sacrifice unto the Lord our God.

26 Our cattle also shall go with us; there shall not an hoof be left behind; for thereof must we take to serve the Lord our God; and we know not with what we must serve the Lord, until we come thither.

27 But the Lord hardened Pharaoh's heart, and he would not let them go.

28 And Pharaoh said unto him, Get thee from me, take heed to thyself, see my face no more; for in that day thou seest my face thou shalt die.

29 And Moses said, Thou hast spoken well, I will see thy face again no more.

John 19:19-22

19 And Pilate wrote a title, and put it on the cross. And the writing was Jesus Of Nazareth The King Of The Jews.

20 This title then read many of the Jews: for the place where Jesus was crucified was nigh to the city: and it was written in Hebrew, and Greek, and Latin.

21 Then said the chief priests of the Jews to Pilate, Write not, The King of the Jews; but that he said, I am King of the Jews.

22 Pilate answered, What I have written I have written.

Matthew 27:54

54 Now when the centurion, and they that were with him, watching Jesus, saw the earthquake, and those things that were done, they feared greatly, saying, Truly this was the Son of God.

Chapter 6

Romans 5:11

11 And not only so, but we also joy in God through our Lord Jesus Christ, by whom we have now received the atonement.

Matthew 26:26-28

26 And as they were eating, Jesus took bread, and blessed it, and brake it, and gave it to the disciples, and said, Take, eat; this is my body.
27 And he took the cup, and gave thanks, and gave it to them, saying, Drink ye all of it;
28 For this is my blood of the new testament, which is shed for many for the remission of sins.

Leviticus 16:17

17 And there shall be no man in the tabernacle of the congregation when he goeth in to make an atonement in the holy place, until he come out, and have made an atonement for himself, and for his household, and for all the congregation of Israel.

Exodus 39:24-26

24 And they made upon the hems of the robe pomegranates of blue, and purple, and scarlet, and twined linen.
25 And they made bells of pure gold, and put the bells between the pomegranates upon the hem of the robe, round about between the pomegranates;
26 A bell and a pomegranate, a bell and a pomegranate, round about the hem of the robe to minister in; as the Lord commanded Moses.

John 3:18

18 He that believeth on him is not condemned: but he that believeth not is condemned already, because he hath not believed in the name of the only begotten Son of God.

John 6:37

37 All that the Father giveth me shall come to me; and him that cometh to me I will in no wise cast out.

1 John 1:9

9 If we confess our sins, he is faithful and just to forgive us our sins, and to cleanse us from all unrighteousness.

Chapter 7

Luke 22:13-20

13 And they went, and found as he had said unto them: and they made ready the passover.
14 And when the hour was come, he sat down, and the twelve apostles with him.
15 And he said unto them, With desire I have desired to eat this passover with you before I suffer:
16 For I say unto you, I will not any more eat thereof, until it be fulfilled in the kingdom of God.
17 And he took the cup, and gave thanks, and said, Take this, and divide it among yourselves:
18 For I say unto you, I will not drink of the fruit of the vine, until the kingdom of God shall come.
19 And he took bread, and gave thanks, and brake it, and gave unto them, saying, This is my body which is given for you: this do in remembrance of me.
20 Likewise also the cup after supper, saying, This cup is the new testament in my blood, which is shed for you.

Matthew 26:26-30

26 And as they were eating, Jesus took bread, and blessed it, and brake it, and gave it to the disciples, and said, Take, eat; this is my body.
27 And he took the cup, and gave thanks, and gave it to them, saying, Drink ye all of it;
28 For this is my blood of the new testament, which is shed for many for the remission of sins.
29 But I say unto you, I will not drink henceforth of this fruit of the vine, until that day when I drink it new with you in my Father's kingdom.
30 And when they had sung an hymn, they went out into the mount of Olives.

1 Corinthians 5:6-8

6 Your glorying is not good. Know ye not that a little leaven leaveneth the whole lump?
7 Purge out therefore the old leaven, that ye may be a new lump, as ye are unleavened. For even Christ our passover is sacrificed for us:
8 Therefore let us keep the feast, not with old leaven, neither with the leaven of malice and wickedness; but with the unleavened bread of sincerity and truth.

1 Corinthians 10:16

16 The cup of blessing which we bless, is it not the communion of the blood of Christ? The bread which we break, is it not the communion of the body of Christ?

Ephesians1:13

13 In whom ye also trusted, after that ye heard the word of truth, the gospel of your salvation: in whom also after that ye believed, ye were sealed with that holy Spirit of promise,

John 4

1 When therefore the Lord knew how the Pharisees had heard that Jesus made and baptized more disciples than John,

2 (Though Jesus himself baptized not, but his disciples,)

3 He left Judaea, and departed again into Galilee.

4 And he must needs go through Samaria.

5 Then cometh he to a city of Samaria, which is called Sychar, near to the parcel of ground that Jacob gave to his son Joseph.

6 Now Jacob's well was there. Jesus therefore, being wearied with his journey, sat thus on the well: and it was about the sixth hour.

7 There cometh a woman of Samaria to draw water: Jesus saith unto her, Give me to drink.

8 (For his disciples were gone away unto the city to buy meat.)

9 Then saith the woman of Samaria unto him, How is it that thou, being a Jew, askest drink of me, which am a woman of Samaria? for the Jews have no dealings with the Samaritans.

10 Jesus answered and said unto her, If thou knewest the gift of God, and who it is that saith to thee, Give me to drink; thou wouldest have asked of him, and he would have given thee living water.

11 The woman saith unto him, Sir, thou hast nothing to draw with, and the well is deep: from whence then hast thou that living water?

12 Art thou greater than our father Jacob, which gave us the well, and drank thereof himself, and his children, and his cattle?

13 Jesus answered and said unto her, Whosoever drinketh of this water shall thirst again:

14 But whosoever drinketh of the water that I shall give him shall never thirst; but the water that I shall give him shall be in him a well of water springing up into everlasting life.

15 The woman saith unto him, Sir, give me this water, that I thirst not, neither come hither to draw.

16 Jesus saith unto her, Go, call thy husband, and come hither.

17 The woman answered and said, I have no husband. Jesus said unto her, Thou hast well said, I have no husband:

18 For thou hast had five husbands; and he whom thou now hast is not thy husband: in that saidst thou truly.

19 The woman saith unto him, Sir, I perceive that thou art a prophet.

20 Our fathers worshipped in this mountain; and ye say, that in Jerusalem is the place where men ought to worship.

21 Jesus saith unto her, Woman, believe me, the hour cometh, when ye shall neither in this mountain, nor yet at Jerusalem, worship the Father.

22 Ye worship ye know not what: we know what we worship: for salvation is of the Jews.

23 But the hour cometh, and now is, when the true worshippers shall worship the Father in spirit and in truth: for the Father seeketh such to worship him.

24 God is a Spirit: and they that worship him must worship him in spirit and in truth.

25 The woman saith unto him, I know that Messias cometh, which is called Christ: when he is come, he will tell us all things.

26 Jesus saith unto her, I that speak unto thee am he.

27 And upon this came his disciples, and marvelled that he talked with the woman: yet no man said, What seekest thou? or, Why talkest thou with her?

28 The woman then left her waterpot, and went her way into the city, and saith to the men,

29 Come, see a man, which told me all things that ever I did: is not this the Christ?

30 Then they went out of the city, and came unto him.

31 In the mean while his disciples prayed him, saying, Master, eat.

32 But he said unto them, I have meat to eat that ye know not of.

33 Therefore said the disciples one to another, Hath any man brought him ought to eat?

34 Jesus saith unto them, My meat is to do the will of him that sent me, and to finish his work.

35 Say not ye, There are yet four months, and then cometh harvest? behold, I say unto you, Lift up your eyes, and look on the fields; for they are white already to harvest.
36 And he that reapeth receiveth wages, and gathereth fruit unto life eternal: that both he that soweth and he that reapeth may rejoice together.
37 And herein is that saying true, One soweth, and another reapeth.
38 I sent you to reap that whereon ye bestowed no labour: other men laboured, and ye are entered into their labours.
39 And many of the Samaritans of that city believed on him for the saying of the woman, which testified, He told me all that ever I did.
40 So when the Samaritans were come unto him, they besought him that he would tarry with them: and he abode there two days.
41 And many more believed because of his own word;
42 And said unto the woman, Now we believe, not because of thy saying: for we have heard him ourselves, and know that this is indeed the Christ, the Saviour of the world.
43 Now after two days he departed thence, and went into Galilee.
44 For Jesus himself testified, that a prophet hath no honour in his own country.
45 Then when he was come into Galilee, the Galilaeans received him, having seen all the things that he did at Jerusalem at the feast: for they also went unto the feast.
46 So Jesus came again into Cana of Galilee, where he made the water wine. And there was a certain nobleman, whose son was sick at Capernaum.
47 When he heard that Jesus was come out of Judaea into Galilee, he went unto him, and besought him that he would come down, and heal his son: for he was at the point of death.
48 Then said Jesus unto him, Except ye see signs and wonders, ye will not believe.
49 The nobleman saith unto him, Sir, come down ere my child die.
50 Jesus saith unto him, Go thy way; thy son liveth. And the man believed the word that Jesus had spoken unto him, and he went his way.
51 And as he was now going down, his servants met him, and told him, saying, Thy son liveth.
52 Then enquired he of them the hour when he began to amend. And they said unto him, Yesterday at the seventh hour the fever left him.
53 So the father knew that it was at the same hour, in the which Jesus said unto him, Thy son liveth: and himself believed, and his whole house.
54 This is again the second miracle that Jesus did, when he was come out of Judaea into Galilee.

James 1:17

17 Every good gift and every perfect gift is from above, and cometh down from the Father of lights, with whom is no variableness, neither shadow of turning.

Micah 7:19

19 He will turn again, he will have compassion upon us; he will subdue our iniquities; and thou wilt cast all their sins into the depths of the sea.

Psalm 103:12

12 As far as the east is from the west, so far hath he removed our transgressions from us.

Exodus 12   (See Chapter One above)

Psalm 113

1 Praise ye the Lord. Praise, O ye servants of the Lord, praise the name of the Lord.
2 Blessed be the name of the Lord from this time forth and for evermore.
3 From the rising of the sun unto the going down of the same the Lord's name is to be praised.
4 The Lord is high above all nations, and his glory above the heavens.
5 Who is like unto the Lord our God, who dwelleth on high,
6 Who humbleth himself to behold the things that are in heaven, and in the earth!
7 He raiseth up the poor out of the dust, and lifteth the needy out of the dunghill;
8 That he may set him with princes, even with the princes of his people.
9 He maketh the barren woman to keep house, and to be a joyful mother of children. Praise ye the Lord.

Psalm 114

1 When Israel went out of Egypt, the house of Jacob from a people of strange language;
2 Judah was his sanctuary, and Israel his dominion.
3 The sea saw it, and fled: Jordan was driven back.
4 The mountains skipped like rams, and the little hills like lambs.
5 What ailed thee, O thou sea, that thou fleddest? thou Jordan, that thou wast driven back?
6 Ye mountains, that ye skipped like rams; and ye little hills, like lambs?
7 Tremble, thou earth, at the presence of the Lord, at the presence of the God of Jacob;
8 Which turned the rock into a standing water, the flint into a fountain of waters.

Psalm 115-Psalm 118

115

1 Not unto us, O Lord, not unto us, but unto thy name give glory, for thy mercy, and for thy truth's sake.
2 Wherefore should the heathen say, Where is now their God?
3 But our God is in the heavens: he hath done whatsoever he hath pleased.
4 Their idols are silver and gold, the work of men's hands.
5 They have mouths, but they speak not: eyes have they, but they see not:
6 They have ears, but they hear not: noses have they, but they smell not:
7 They have hands, but they handle not: feet have they, but they walk not: neither speak they through their throat.
8 They that make them are like unto them; so is every one that trusteth in them.
9 O Israel, trust thou in the Lord: he is their help and their shield.
10 O house of Aaron, trust in the Lord: he is their help and their shield.
11 Ye that fear the Lord, trust in the Lord: he is their help and their shield.
12 The Lord hath been mindful of us: he will bless us; he will bless the house of Israel; he will bless the house of Aaron.
13 He will bless them that fear the Lord, both small and great.
14 The Lord shall increase you more and more, you and your children.
15 Ye are blessed of the Lord which made heaven and earth.
16 The heaven, even the heavens, are the Lord's: but the earth hath he given to the children of men.
17 The dead praise not the Lord, neither any that go down into silence.

18 But we will bless the Lord from this time forth and for evermore. Praise the Lord.

116

1 I love the Lord, because he hath heard my voice and my supplications.
2 Because he hath inclined his ear unto me, therefore will I call upon him as long as I live.
3 The sorrows of death compassed me, and the pains of hell gat hold upon me: I found trouble and sorrow.
4 Then called I upon the name of the Lord; O Lord, I beseech thee, deliver my soul.
5 Gracious is the Lord, and righteous; yea, our God is merciful.
6 The Lord preserveth the simple: I was brought low, and he helped me.
7 Return unto thy rest, O my soul; for the Lord hath dealt bountifully with thee.
8 For thou hast delivered my soul from death, mine eyes from tears, and my feet from falling.
9 I will walk before the Lord in the land of the living.
10 I believed, therefore have I spoken: I was greatly afflicted:
11 I said in my haste, All men are liars.
12 What shall I render unto the Lord for all his benefits toward me?
13 I will take the cup of salvation, and call upon the name of the Lord.
14 I will pay my vows unto the Lord now in the presence of all his people.
15 Precious in the sight of the Lord is the death of his saints.
16 O Lord, truly I am thy servant; I am thy servant, and the son of thine handmaid: thou hast loosed my bonds.
17 I will offer to thee the sacrifice of thanksgiving, and will call upon the name of the Lord.
18 I will pay my vows unto the Lord now in the presence of all his people.
19 In the courts of the Lord's house, in the midst of thee, O Jerusalem. Praise ye the Lord.

117

1 O praise the Lord, all ye nations: praise him, all ye people.
2 For his merciful kindness is great toward us: and the truth of the Lord endureth for ever. Praise ye the Lord.

118

1 O give thanks unto the Lord; for he is good: because his mercy endureth for ever.
2 Let Israel now say, that his mercy endureth for ever.
3 Let the house of Aaron now say, that his mercy endureth for ever.
4 Let them now that fear the Lord say, that his mercy endureth for ever.
5 I called upon the Lord in distress: the Lord answered me, and set me in a large place.
6 The Lord is on my side; I will not fear: what can man do unto me?
7 The Lord taketh my part with them that help me: therefore shall I see my desire upon them that hate me.
8 It is better to trust in the Lord than to put confidence in man.
9 It is better to trust in the Lord than to put confidence in princes.
10 All nations compassed me about: but in the name of the Lord will I destroy them.
11 They compassed me about; yea, they compassed me about: but in the name of the Lord I will destroy them.
12 They compassed me about like bees: they are quenched as the fire of thorns: for in the name of the Lord I will destroy them.

13 Thou hast thrust sore at me that I might fall: but the Lord helped me.

14 The Lord is my strength and song, and is become my salvation.

15 The voice of rejoicing and salvation is in the tabernacles of the righteous: the right hand of the Lord doeth valiantly.

16 The right hand of the Lord is exalted: the right hand of the Lord doeth valiantly.

17 I shall not die, but live, and declare the works of the Lord.

18 The Lord hath chastened me sore: but he hath not given me over unto death.

19 Open to me the gates of righteousness: I will go into them, and I will praise the Lord:

20 This gate of the Lord, into which the righteous shall enter.

21 I will praise thee: for thou hast heard me, and art become my salvation.

22 The stone which the builders refused is become the head stone of the corner.

23 This is the Lord's doing; it is marvellous in our eyes.

24 This is the day which the Lord hath made; we will rejoice and be glad in it.

25 Save now, I beseech thee, O Lord: O Lord, I beseech thee, send now prosperity.

26 Blessed be he that cometh in the name of the Lord: we have blessed you out of the house of the Lord.

27 God is the Lord, which hath shewed us light: bind the sacrifice with cords, even unto the horns of the altar.

28 Thou art my God, and I will praise thee: thou art my God, I will exalt thee.

29 O give thanks unto the Lord; for he is good: for his mercy endureth for ever.

Psalm 75:8

8 For in the hand of the Lord there is a cup, and the wine is red; it is full of mixture; and he poureth out of the same: but the dregs thereof, all the wicked of the earth shall wring them out, and drink them.

1 Corinthians 11:24-25

24 And when he had given thanks, he brake it, and said, Take, eat: this is my body, which is broken for you: this do in remembrance of me.

25 After the same manner also he took the cup, when he had supped, saying, this cup is the new testament in my blood: this do ye, as oft as ye drink it, in remembrance of me.

Chapter 8

Matthew 1:21

1 And she shall bring forth a son, and thou shalt call his name Jesus: for he shall save his people from their sins.

1 Peter 1:18-20

18 Forasmuch as ye know that ye were not redeemed with corruptible things, as silver and gold, from your vain conversation received by tradition from your fathers;

19 But with the precious blood of Christ, as of a lamb without blemish and without spot:

20 Who verily was foreordained before the foundation of the world, but was manifest in these last times for you.

Romans 5:6-10

6 For when we were yet without strength, in due time Christ died for the ungodly.
7 For scarcely for a righteous man will one die: yet peradventure for a good man some would even dare to die.
8 But God commendeth his love toward us, in that, while we were yet sinners, Christ died for us.
9 Much more then, being now justified by his blood, we shall be saved from wrath through him.
10 For if, when we were enemies, we were reconciled to God by the death of his Son, much more, being reconciled, we shall be saved by his life.

Galatians 1:3-5

3 Grace be to you and peace from God the Father, and from our Lord Jesus Christ,
4 Who gave himself for our sins, that he might deliver us from this present evil world, according to the will of God and our Father:
5 To whom be glory for ever and ever. Amen

Colossians 2:15

15 And having spoiled principalities and powers, he made a shew of them openly, triumphing over them in it.

Galatians 6:14

14 But God forbid that I should glory, save in the cross of our Lord Jesus Christ, by whom the world is crucified unto me, and I unto the world.

1 Peter 1:18-20 (see above)

2 Peter 2:4

4 For if God spared not the angels that sinned, but cast them down to hell, and delivered them into chains of darkness, to be reserved unto judgment;

Romans 6:23

23 For the wages of sin is death; but the gift of God is eternal life through Jesus Christ our Lord.

Galatians 2:10

10 Only they would that we should remember the poor; the same which I also was forward to do.

Matthew 1:21 (see above)

John 17:2, 6, 9-11, 24

2 As thou hast given him power over all flesh, that he should give eternal life to as many as thou hast given him.

6 I have manifested thy name unto the men which thou gavest me out of the world: thine they were, and thou gavest them me; and they have kept thy word.
9 I pray for them: I pray not for the world, but for them which thou hast given me; for they are thine.
10 And all mine are thine, and thine are mine; and I am glorified in them.
11 And now I am no more in the world, but these are in the world, and I come to thee. Holy Father, keep through thine own name those whom thou hast given me, that they may be one, as we are.
24 Father, I will that they also, whom thou hast given me, be with me where I am; that they may behold my glory, which thou hast given me: for thou lovedst me before the foundation of the world

Matthew 1:21 (see above)

John 6:37 (see above)

John 6:39

39 And this is the Father's will which hath sent me, that of all which he hath given me I should lose nothing, but should raise it up again at the last day.

John 10:15

15 As the Father knoweth me, even so know I the Father: and I lay down my life for the sheep.

John 15:13

13 Greater love hath no man than this, that a man lay down his life for his friends.

Acts 20:28

28 Take heed therefore unto yourselves, and to all the flock, over the which the Holy Ghost hath made you overseers, to feed the church of God, which he hath purchased with his own blood.

Romans 8:33

33 Who shall lay any thing to the charge of God's elect? It is God that justifieth.

1 Peter 1:2

2 Elect according to the foreknowledge of God the Father, through sanctification of the Spirit, unto obedience and sprinkling of the blood of Jesus Christ: Grace unto you, and peace, be multiplied.

Galatians 6:14 (see above)

Chapter 9

Psalm 111:9

9 He sent redemption unto his people: he hath commanded his covenant for ever: holy and reverend is his name.

Colossians 1:21-21

12 Giving thanks unto the Father, which hath made us meet to be partakers of the inheritance of the saints in light:
13 Who hath delivered us from the power of darkness, and hath translated us into the kingdom of his dear Son:
14 In whom we have redemption through his blood, even the forgiveness of sins:
15 Who is the image of the invisible God, the firstborn of every creature:
16 For by him were all things created, that are in heaven, and that are in earth, visible and invisible, whether they be thrones, or dominions, or principalities, or powers: all things were created by him, and for him:
17 And he is before all things, and by him all things consist.
18 And he is the head of the body, the church: who is the beginning, the firstborn from the dead; that in all things he might have the preeminence.
19 For it pleased the Father that in him should all fulness dwell;
20 And, having made peace through the blood of his cross, by him to reconcile all things unto himself; by him, I say, whether they be things in earth, or things in heaven.
21 And you, that were sometime alienated and enemies in your mind by wicked works, yet now hath he reconciled.

Hebrews 9:12

12 Neither by the blood of goats and calves, but by his own blood he entered in once into the holy place, having obtained eternal redemption for us.

Ephesians 1:7

7 In whom we have redemption through his blood, the forgiveness of sins, according to the riches of his grace.

Hebrews 9:12 (see above)

Colossians1:14

14 In whom we have redemption through his blood, even the forgiveness of sins.

1 Peter 1:18-25

18 Forasmuch as ye know that ye were not redeemed with corruptible things, as silver and gold, from your vain conversation received by tradition from your fathers;
19 But with the precious blood of Christ, as of a lamb without blemish and without spot:

20 Who verily was foreordained before the foundation of the world, but was manifest in these last times for you,

21 Who by him do believe in God, that raised him up from the dead, and gave him glory; that your faith and hope might be in God.

22 Seeing ye have purified your souls in obeying the truth through the Spirit unto unfeigned love of the brethren, see that ye love one another with a pure heart fervently:

23 Being born again, not of corruptible seed, but of incorruptible, by the word of God, which liveth and abideth for ever.

24 For all flesh is as grass, and all the glory of man as the flower of grass. The grass withereth, and the flower thereof falleth away:

25 But the word of the Lord endureth for ever. And this is the word which by the gospel is preached unto you.

1 Corinthians 1:30

30 But of him are ye in Christ Jesus, who of God is made unto us wisdom, and righteousness, and sanctification, and redemption:

Romans 5:6-10

6 For when we were yet without strength, in due time Christ died for the ungodly.

7 For scarcely for a righteous man will one die: yet peradventure for a good man some would even dare to die.

8 But God commendeth his love toward us, in that, while we were yet sinners, Christ died for us.

9 Much more then, being now justified by his blood, we shall be saved from wrath through him.

10 For if, when we were enemies, we were reconciled to God by the death of his Son, much more, being reconciled, we shall be saved by his life.

Luke 23:33

33 And when they were come to the place, which is called Calvary, there they crucified him, and the malefactors, one on the right hand, and the other on the left.

Galatians 1:3-5

3 Grace be to you and peace from God the Father, and from our Lord Jesus Christ,

4 Who gave himself for our sins, that he might deliver us from this present evil world, according to the will of God and our Father:

5 To whom be glory for ever and ever. Amen.

1 Peter 1:18-21 (see above)

1 Peter 1:20 (see above)

CPSIA information can be obtained
at www.ICGtesting.com
Printed in the USA
FFOW04n0318100218
45028139-45378FF